Fifty Tails of Grey

Tina K Burton & Paul L Burton

Foreword by Uri Geller

This book is dedicated to the numerous greyhounds who've had or are leading unhappy lives, they deserve better. It's too late to help those already departed, but we hope that all present and future hounds find love and kindness, and will eventually run free and happy at the Rainbow Bridge.

We'd like to thank all our greyhound owning friends, many from our Facebook group, who contributed and shared their stories, and the volunteers from across the world, who give up their time and money to help these wonderful dogs.

Thank you to my husband Paul for designing the cover, and for doing everything else involved in publishing this book.

Special thanks to Uri Geller for providing the foreword.

We hope you'll enjoy reading how we all came to share our lives with our greys, and that it'll encourage you to rehome one yourselves. These are real stories, written by greyhound owners, in their own words, all I did was edit them and put them together.

The proceeds from the sale of this book will be shared between two greyhound rescue charities.

Tina K Burton

Foreword

I was two-years old when my father brought home a puppy in a shoe box. I instantly became a dog lover.
All my life I had dogs of different breeds, but when we got our rescue greyhound I felt that he was a special dog. Greyhounds have a unique, deep, loving energy that they emanate and transmit.
One can physically absorb that unconditional love.
I recommend this book to every animal lover.

Uri Geller

Cherry's Story - Tina K Burton

In July 2014, I was reading a book by my writing friend, Chris Stovell. The main character had a greyhound called Gracie. I loved the sound of her, and for some reason, right out of the blue, I decided we should have one.

We'd never owned a dog before, let alone a greyhound, and my husband Paul was adamant we weren't having any more pets. Our two cats were no longer with us, and he didn't want the responsibility of another animal. But, my sixth sense was telling me this was something we should do.

We are both home all day - my husband is retired, and I'm a writer - so, we had the time to devote to a dog. I cajoled and pleaded with him until he finally agreed, and we then spent some time looking up information about greyhounds. We knew absolutely nothing about them, but wanted to find out as much as we could. The more we researched, the more we realised they'd be the perfect dog for us. They make fantastic pets because, contrary to what people think, they don't require a lot of exercise. Their favourite past-time is roaching - lying on their backs with their legs akimbo - on a sofa. They are gentle, sensitive souls, and are ideal for the elderly, as well as families. They also, apparently, don't bark a lot.

I went on the Retired Greyhound Trust's website, and whilst browsing the photos of all the dogs who needed a home, I saw a pretty female greyhound called Cherry. She wasn't yet two-years old, which was quite unusual. They're normally older dogs, given up for rehoming after their racing careers have ended.

Paul liked the look of her too, so we planned to visit Cherry the following day, on our way to stay with relatives. I was so excited. I'd had pets of my own before - guinea pigs and chinchillas for my daughter when she was little, and cats, but I'd never had a dog.

When the volunteer opened the cage door, Cherry ran out, jumped up at Paul, and licked him all over his face. We knew then that she was the dog for us.

We had to wait a while for a home check to be done, which we thankfully passed, and we collected Cherry two days later.

She'd never lived in a house before, and we'd never had a dog, so we learned everything together. That first day, after walking her around the house on a lead, we let her off to explore in her own time. She went upstairs, and then panicked because with those long legs, she didn't know how to get back down again. Paul had to go up and help her.

That night, we thought she'd be safe sleeping in the hallway, and we left the kitchen door open so she could go in and get a drink if she wanted. What we hadn't remembered was that she's the perfect height for 'counter surfing.'

Not long after going up to bed, we heard an almighty crash. Cherry had jumped up at the work surface, and knocked off two wine glasses we'd foolishly left at the back of it. Thankfully, she wasn't hurt, but it was a lesson well learned!

We didn't get much sleep for the rest of that night because she howled and cried for hours.

When you think about it, she'd been taken away from everything she knew, to an unfamiliar place, with complete strangers. No wonder she was upset. But, we survived. The next day, our neighbours lent us a stair gate, which we put at the entrance to our bedroom, so we could leave the door open. We'd closed it the night before, so poor Cherry hadn't been able to see us, and for a dog who's had company her whole life so far - either humans or other greyhounds - she must have felt scared and alone. We hadn't even thought about that aspect, and I felt terrible. But she could see us now and was much happier. She slept right through that night.

She had so many things to get used to. She didn't know what all the usual household noises were, like the TV, vacuum cleaner or washing machine, she didn't know how to play, or even what her own name was. She wolfed down her food because she'd always had to compete for meals and didn't understand that the dish of food I put down was just for her and wouldn't be eaten by anyone else, or taken away.

Her world was all new and a bit scary, but with time, patience and love, we got there. She took almost everything in her stride; hardly anything seemed to worry or faze her. The only things she doesn't like are very loud noises and especially gunshots. We live in the countryside and, unfortunately, there's quite a lot of shooting, which terrifies the poor dog to the point that she screams. On one occasion we'd gone to the forest for a walk and as we opened the boot to get her out, she heard gunshots. There was no way we could get her out of the car. She climbed over the back seats, and then tried to get over the front seats in her desperation to get away. It makes you wonder what on earth has happened in her past to make such a normally outgoing dog so scared.

She loves going out in the car, and will jump into the boot quite happily as soon as we open it. In fact, she loves car journeys so much; she'll get in anyone's open car. Our friends came to stay with us for a long weekend, and when they arrived, and Tony got out of the car, he left the door open. Quick as a shot, Cherry jumped in and made herself comfortable. I don't think Tony was too happy about a dog sitting in the front seat of his precious car, ha ha.

Over a year on, we've learned so much. Cherry has blossomed - see what I did there? - And we've got a beautiful, gentle, sensitive, fun and sometimes crazy hound, who we love to bits. And she still hasn't barked, which is great as I'm not keen on noisy dogs!

I believe that everything happens for a reason, and I think we were meant to be together. Fate gave us a helping hand that summer's day by choosing that book for me to read.

Arik's Story - Sara Mortimer

Once I was a racer,
Running round a track,
I kept my focus on the lure,
I wasn't looking back.
The people cheered and praised me,
They said I could run fast,
But then other dogs got faster,
And I started to come last.
What would happen to me now?
I'd committed the Great Sin,
Other dogs had told me,
'All you need to do is win!'
I knew my trainer loved me,
He'd called me his Livewire,
But still he came to tell me,
'You're going to retire.'
I saw his disappointment,
Tears made his eyes gleam,
I suddenly felt very scared,
What did 'retiring' mean?
Could I not just run one more race?
Just give me one more chance?
But people put me in a van,
Without a backward glance.
So what would happen to me now?
Where do retired dogs go?
I asked the others in the van,
But no-one seemed to know.
The van stopped, the doors opened,
The sign said 'RGT,'
And I saw lots of other hounds,
Race losers, just like me.
I settled in my kennel,
Became part of the routine,
Was this to be my life now?
Is this what retiring means?
People came to see us,

9

Some took my friends away,
But no-one ever called my name,
So it was just another day.
This was my life for a whole year,
Just food, sleep and a walk,
Please don't ask me how I am,
I just don't want to talk.
Then one day I hear your voice,
'I want a boy you see...'
I look up from my feeding bowl,
And you're looking straight at me!
Suddenly I'm happy,
Your look brings me pure joy,
'Oh please take me away with you,
I want to be your boy!'
I jump up, I must touch you,
Your white coat meets my paws,
I'm sorry I am muddy,
But I really must be yours!
You take me for a short walk,
I can't keep in a straight line,
I'm simply too excited,
To have you by my side.
We head back to the kennels,
And I am led away,
'No please don't say I've blown it,
Please tell me that you'll stay.'
Weeks pass and I don't see you,
My mind is in a fog,
My muddy paws have ruined it,
You chose another dog.
And then one day I hear you,
I hear you ask for me,
You've come back for a cuddle,
You've come to set me free!
Three hours we are together,
I've never been so hugged and kissed,
So is this what retiring is?
Is this what I've missed?

Then you say you have to go again,
But what did I do wrong?
And what exactly do you mean,
When you say you 'won't be long?'
So I go back to my kennel,
What else can I do?
Can't I make you understand,
I want to be with you?
A few weeks pass without you,
My heart has really cried,
The other dogs just look at me,
'We all know that you tried.'
So this is my retirement then?
I just don't have a choice,
I guess I'll ...Wait a minute,
I can hear your voice!
This time you sound different,
You ask 'Where do I sign?'
You place a collar round my neck,
Then tell me, 'You are mine!'
Now I have a new coat on,
And I'm getting in your car.
I don't know where I'm going,
But I'm guessing it's quite far,
I sit down by the back seat,
You sit by my side.
I can see out all the windows,
Wow, this is quite a ride!
We're getting on a ferry,
We're crossing a big sea,
Do you really mean to tell me,
You came all this way for Me?
I've been with you for years now,
I'm with you every day,
We do everything together,
So I know I'm here to stay.
You let me on the sofa,
We have cuddles on your bed,
I love your arms around me,

As you stroke and kiss my head.
I'm settled. You have changed me,
Your mum says I've changed you.
I know you're always there for me,
And I'm here for you too.
The moment I jumped up at you,
Is what played the biggest part,
I wasn't aiming for your coat,
I was aiming for your heart.

Hare and Merlin's Story - Karen Collins

We decided we'd like a family dog, so we started looking for one for my son who has autism, and my daughter, who wanted a small, fluffy cute puppy of some kind.

We tried some of the rehoming centres but couldn't find one we all liked.

Then, by chance, I heard that greyhounds make lovely pets. I must admit I wasn't sure - they're rather large and bony - but the following weekend we headed to our local garden centre because the nearby Retired Greyhound Trust kennels had brought a few greyhounds for people to meet.

My son loved them. He was laughing and smiling away, which was a good sign for us. So just a week later, we found ourselves at Greyhound Homer, being introduced to several hounds. My son didn't seem interested in any of them and I was beginning to doubt that we'd find one he liked, but then a little black and white girl calmly walked up to him. He stroked her head and she nuzzled him. It was lovely to watch, and we knew then that she was the one for us.

We had to get our garden fenced repaired, but we passed the home check, and just two weeks after first seeing Hare, we went to collect her.

Well what a first few days we had with her! My son insisted on taking her to his school to meet all his friends, and she soon took over the bed, sofa - a sofa is a must-have for greyhounds - chairs and our lives. BBQs are also a firm favourite of hers.

She changed our lives for the better, and my son's talking and social skills really improved.

We noticed however that even though I'm home all day, Hare followed me like a shadow, and liked the company of other dogs, so just four months later, Merlin came home too.

Someone had posted a cry for help on Facebook. His foster mum couldn't look after him anymore, and was worried that he'd have to go back to kennels. I looked at my husband who sighed, then said, 'Yes okay, we'll go and meet him.'

He travelled down with my daughter and Hare, and all four were soon back home.

There were initially a few teething troubles as Merlin and

Hare settled down together, but after two weeks they became firm friends. Merlin isn't keen on small dogs or cats, but the daft dog is very protective of...the hamster!

Small fluffy and cute? Nope. But the most loyal and loving dogs I've known? Yes.

Now the only question remains, when are we getting number three?

Frosty's Story - Amy O'Connor

When we first went to pick our greyhound, my granddad and I were a little bit sceptical about it, however meeting Frosty completely changed that.

We went to North Yorkshire Retired Greyhound Trust kennels one Saturday, and Tom - who ran the kennels - picked out twelve hounds for us to look at.

When the first six came out, five of them were running around sniffing and having fun, and the other one just came and stood by the side of my granddad for a stroke, and that trademark leaning on you that they do.

Tom put those ones back in and brought out the next six, who also ran around sniffing everything.

We just couldn't decide between them; they were all nice, so we asked for the first six to be brought back out again. The same five ran around, and the same one came plodding up to my granddad and leaned on him. We realized at this point that we hadn't gone to choose a hound, we'd gone for a hound to choose us, and the one stood leaning on my granddad had quite clearly decided he was coming home with us.

That hound was our daft, lazy, cheeky Frosty.

The kennel staff were reluctant to let him come home with us that same day, because he'd broken a leg in his last race and was still under the vet, but after a little bit of pleading, and agreeing to take him back for his vet visits, we were allowed to take him.

What was the first thing he did when he got in the house? He plonked himself on his bed and pretty much didn't move for ten years, ha ha.

Sadly we lost Frosty at the age of thirteen, and we miss him every single day. He was our best friend, and the most deserving master we have ever served.

Sylvia's Story - Victoria Hanman

Several years ago, I dreamt that I was stroking the soft shiny head of a fawn greyhound called Pudding. When I woke up, all I could remember were those soulful eyes looking up at me and feeling immense love. I let the dream slip to the back of my mind, but it never disappeared.

Fast forward to 7 July 2008. My day started as normal. At work sitting at my desk I had a thought, today was the day I was going to get myself a greyhound! So I started the search. Never having a pooch before or knowing anything about greyhounds, I logged onto Preloved. There was an advert for a greyhound free to a good home in York. As I'm in the Midlands, it was a little far to travel, but me being me, I called the number and spoke to a lovely man called Bill* who told me he had two greyhounds who needed rehoming, both of which had refused to race. I preferred the sound of the girl, Kexby* Sylvia. I explained that I lived in a flat on the top floor of an old manor house next to my parents' fields, and while it wasn't ideal, she would have plenty of fenced in exercise space.

We agreed to meet later that afternoon at Ferrybridge Services. I was nervous with excitement, yet scared too, what had I let myself in for? Off I and my boyfriend at the time set, wondering what we were going to call her. I was quite taken with the names Pudding or Treacle. When we arrived and met Bill, he opened the back of his van and out the dog hopped. A little scared and slightly shaking, she plonked herself on the back seat of my car. I was amazed at how big she was! I signed the paperwork and asked Bill the usual newbie questions. Then off we set. All the way home, she didn't raise her head and carried on shaking. It was on the way back that we decided the name Sylvia actually quite suited her.

On arrival at my flat, it was apparent that she couldn't walk up stairs, so for three long weeks, she was carried up and down three flights of stairs. Life with Sylvia wasn't as I'd expected. I was young and naive, assuming that you had a dog and it knew its name and basic commands. Me and Sylvia weren't getting on that well, she preferred my boyfriend to me. There were several times
in the first month that I regretted my decision and seriously thought about returning her.

However, over time, my love for Sylv, as I called her, began to grow. And grow it did. She became my shadow and I hers. Wherever I went she came too. A year later my boyfriend and I parted - for the best – and he tried to take Sylvia with him. But there was no way on this earth that was going to happen. During this time, there were a lot of dark days, with no reason to get up or get dressed. However having Sylv to look after made sure I did get up every morning. It was me and Sylvia against the world, and we did just fine.

Eventually we found a new daddy for her, and most recently, Marley - another greyhound - came to live with us. As much as she doesn't like to admit it, she adores him and always looks after him like any good big sister would. Seven years have now passed since that day I headed off up the A1 to collect Sylvia, and every day that goes past I cherish with all my heart. I never knew it was possible to love something so much, we know each other so well, just from one look we both know what each other is thinking, and I truly believe she's my soul mate. As much as I'd love to have Sylvia by my side until my passing day, it breaks my heart to know that at some point the Rainbow Bridge will call her. Last week I dreamt again of being the proud owner of another greyhound, no name this time, just a shiny black coat with white speckles…Watch this space!

Blue's Story - Sarah Tyrrell Jones

In the school summer holidays of 2007, it was just me and my son Joseph aged seven. I was going through a divorce, totally broke, and lonely. The loneliness was awful. It ate up every part of me. During the day I had my brave face on for my son, but at night I felt like I was sinking.

I needed to go shopping, so Joe and I got into the clapped out Volvo that my dad had bought us, and went into town. We didn't go the usual way, in fact we went via a village totally out of our way, but something made me drive there.

Joe said, 'Mum what's in the bin bag we just passed?'

I hadn't noticed it, but I pulled up and reversed back. I told Joe to stay in the car while I pulled the bin bag out from hedge. As I did, it moved.

'Whooahh,' Joe shouted.

I ripped the bag open, and inside was a tiny puppy. He was so dirty, I wasn't even sure what colour or breed he was.

What broke my heart was that some cruel person had tied his back legs together with tape. I pulled it off, which made the puppy whine, but he licked me too.

I put him straight onto Joe's lap and we drove to the vets. Joe's little face was a mixture of sadness, yet awe that we had found a puppy.

The vet said the dog was about six-weeks old, and looked to be half Alsatian, half greyhound. He was given some injections, but we were told he may not make it.

We took him home and rang my mum, who came to our house with blankets and tins of baby rice pudding, which the puppy ate off the spoon; his instinct for survival was so strong.

We bathed him, and underneath the dirt we discovered he had a beautiful coat, tiny teeth, and soft paws.

I called him Blue, after the blue hanky we'd found in the bin bag. He's eight-years old now and is strong and very clever. He still sleeps next to me every night. He's my protector and soul mate.

A lot of people say how I saved Blue. But in actual fact, Blue saved me.

Annie's Story - Pauline Presley

I already had one greyhound called Winnie and one elderly short haired pointer, and knew when the pointer finally went over the Rainbow Bridge that I'd get another greyhound as I'd discovered, regardless of the love I felt for all my past dogs, greyhounds have that extra special ingredient that make you want at least one, preferably more, in your lives forever.

One day, while browsing the rescue sites as normal, I saw a photograph of Annie. She was in rescue kennels in Ireland, and they were appealing for someone to adopt her who'd be happy that she couldn't walk very far due to an untreated broken hock. Apparently this damage was sustained very early in her racing life, and being very fast she was put into a breeding pen. She'd been kept there for eight years until she became barren, and then she was discarded.

At the time, Winnie had bad corns, and also couldn't walk very far, so this seemed like a match made in heaven. We didn't intend to get another grey just then, but something about Annie called to us and so I made a phone call.

I was ecstatic to hear we could adopt her, and eagerly awaited the day she was to travel to me. The kennels also noted she had a problem with her shoulder, and after a vet visit to have x-rays, the rescue were told it may be cancer. We were distraught but said we'd have her anyway.

Unfortunately, the week she was due to be spayed she came into season so I agreed to take her un-neutered and have her spayed as soon as the timing was right.

She travelled across to England, and went to kennels in Bristol for the night and we collected her the next day. It was love at first sight!

The following week after she'd settled in, we took her to our vet for a check up as her walking was really laboured. She couldn't walk for more than a few yards before stopping. Luckily my vet at the time was very greyhound savvy and gave her a thorough examination before declaring she was convinced there was no cancer in the shoulder, but in actual fact she had sustained a terrific beating, which had resulted in a badly fractured shoulder. Over a period of time this had calcified, meaning she had no flexibility in her shoulder. Her hock was twisted outward too, so she couldn't reach the floor with that foot, hence the excessive limp. When she was neutered a couple of months later, the vet did a biopsy and took x-rays, which confirmed no cancer, but extremely bad damage. The vet also felt she was not walking because of the terrific pain, so put her on a daily course of painkillers. This made a huge difference, and with encouragement to overcome the psychological side, Annie was eventually happy to walk a much greater distance, at one point even walking a two-mile circuit with many other greyhounds for support.

Understandably Annie had a lot of fears. Fear of men, fear of loud voices, and fear of anyone holding something as though they may hit her. If any of these things happened, the poor girl would wet herself. Over time though she realised she was now safe. Most of her fears remained, but we could easily manage them. In the home and in her own garden, she was joyful - no fear, just love.

Sadly Annie contracted cancer in the damaged shoulder after being with us for a little over two years, and it was extremely aggressive. We lost her a fortnight after the diagnosis.
She was, and always will be, a very special hound in my heart. She endured so much brutality at the hands of humans, but recognised love when she found it and returned that love a thousand fold. It's coming up for four years since we lost her, but even as I type this the tears flow. Annie, I miss you so much. You are always in my thoughts.

Brock's Story - Jeannie Davison

Although I'd grown up with terriers, once I set up my own home, I had cats and never anticipated that one day I'd get a dog of my own.

A few years ago however, greyhounds started appearing in my life. A friend was a fan and I sponsored a rescue greyhound for him as a gift. At a friend's afternoon tea party another guest brought her rescue hound, and my fourteen-year-old son fell in love with his placid nature and big brown eyes.

And so conversations at home turned to getting a dog. A Labrador would need too much exercise to fit into our busy lives. A puppy would need too much attention. But a rescue greyhound...Now, people buy houses online, meet partners online and I set about searching the internet for a cat friendly hound.

Very soon I saw Brock - a big black boy with a gentle face, who'd been waiting for a home at a local Retired Greyhound Trust kennels for a while. Nervously I made contact to see if we could meet him, and a few days later we found ourselves greeting this gentle Irish giant who'd finished his racing career quite some time earlier. My son took him for a brief walk around the track, which was interesting. Brock didn't know his name, wasn't sure how to walk on a lead and seemed more interested in inspecting the track than in making a good impression on some prospective owners.

But make a good impression he did, and a week or so later, we collected him and brought him home.

Panting nervously, he circled the living room, staring and salivating when one of our cats walked into the room. I began to think that we'd made a terrible mistake - he seemed far more interested in having a cat for a snack than in his own treats or new toys.

Tentatively over the next few weeks he began to get used to them, and they to him. He'd dolefully look at us when a cat entered the room, seeming to appreciate that these two furry creatures were way ahead of him in the pack. He learned to come downstairs by himself - getting up was no problem, the descent slightly more problematic - and that the big greyhound in the mirror in my bedroom wasn't a new greyhound friend.

Almost two years on, Brock is the focal point of our home. Everyone gravitates towards him and smothers him with love, even our cats who like to lie beside him, sniffing his snout and trying to clean his ears.

His waggy tailed greeting after a day at work is almost worth going to work for, and his big knowing eyes really do seem like the windows to his gentle soul.

He is well known in the area. When out and about on his walks, or trotting past a busy bus stop, he loves a captive audience and the look on his face when a wild rabbit scampers across his path is priceless. His expression says, 'I've retired now, don't you know?'

Ballymac Marie's Story - Hilary Johnson

Sadly, far too many Irish-bred greyhounds are not smiled upon by Lady Luck, but our Ballymac Marie was most certainly an exception. She had the great good fortune when young to fall into the hands of star trainer Norah McEllistrim, in whose care she spent almost her entire racing career.

When, after 96 races and a respectable track record, she was retired, Norah kept her and Marie moved from the racing kennels into the yard office and on to its leather sofa. There she passed her days pleasantly, apart from on occasion being required to bring an overly macho boy into line. She was quite a bossy little girl.

For a few years, that was that - until one day we came along offering to take one of the homing kennels dogs out on a charity walk with our boy, Darius. As the kennel hounds were all taken, Marie was brought out of the racing kennels next door for this treat. Well, so far as my husband John was concerned, it was love at first sight. He was smitten. The four of us enjoyed a lovely walk in the grounds of a Surrey stately home, on the most beautiful September day.

Back home in Norfolk next day, over coffee in the garden, John said, 'Do you think Norah would let us have Marie?' It wasn't quite that simple. Norah, despite having 40-odd dogs in her charge and another clutch of retired ones at home, loved Marie and wasn't sure if we would cope with such a bossy little madam. And anyway, we didn't want to tear her from Norah's unwilling bosom.

But, to cut it all short, Norah decided that we were okay people to have Marie, reasoning that if we did, then another dog could come into the office. And so, in 2007, she came to live with us. It was rough on poor Darius to begin with, but they soon settled down, and Marie realised that she didn't have to snarl at him if he made his bed, or scratched, or accidentally touched her with a toe.

John adored her. He loved Darius, too, as he had loved all our dogs, but Marie was special. When, in 2010, his health began to fail, she became even more important to him. In 2011, he went into hospital for what, unexpectedly, turned out to be the last time. He died, following an operation, of a cardiac arrest. Shocked, I went into the ward to collect his belongings, and the male nurse handed me a photograph of Marie and Darius. 'He was talking about his dogs just this morning,' he said.

Marie lived for three more years, being put to sleep when she suffered kidney failure three days short of her fourteenth birthday. She had no teeth by then, but she lost none of her spirit or what Norah called her 'little ways'. My beloved Darius died a few months later, the last of the dogs I'd had with John during almost fifty years. I have other hounds in my life now and I love them dearly, but I will always be grateful to the little monkey, Marie, for the joy she brought to John's final years and the comfort she and Darius gave me after he'd gone.

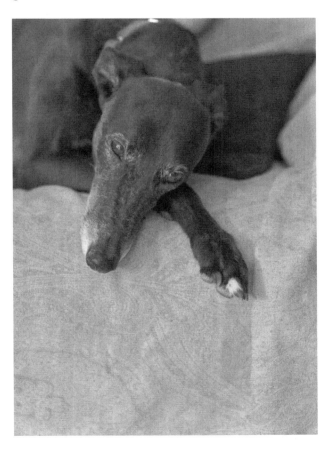

Bruno and Princess's Story - Nick Cornelius

It wasn't meant to happen the way that it did.

We'd lost our old black and tan mongrel, Jack, a few years earlier and it had taken a long time for the family to get over it, especially me.

My wife had said, 'Never again,' but I always knew that it was just a matter of time.

She had a part-time job working as a carer and through this she had met a lady with a greyhound.

She told me how docile and gentle this greyhound was and that the lady used to take her to lots of places to raise awareness of, and funds for, retired greyhounds.

I'd never really thought about greyhounds that much. I knew they raced, I knew where several stadiums were, and I knew that Annette Crosbie had them as pets, but that was all.

This was my chance to get my better half to consider another dog, but not something large like a greyhound, something small and scruffy, that wouldn't require much looking after.

Although I didn't intend to get one, I spent a lot of time reading up about greyhounds on the internet, and got a few books from the library. It was strange really, but my interest had been piqued.

We visited the local Dogs Trust and RSPCA homes and saw lots of dogs, all needing a good home, but nothing really appealed to me. Instead of heading home, we stopped off for a cuppa and a chat.

My wife said that maybe we should visit the greyhound rehoming centre where her 'service user' had got her dog from.

I admitted that I loved the look of them and would like a blue one, but it was a long way from small and scruffy!

The next day we headed out to Whittingham Retired Greyhound Trust kennels in Waltham Abbey.

The kennels were out in the middle of nowhere, at the end of a fairly dodgy track.

They were nothing like the kennels at the Dogs Trust. These were very basic concrete affairs with a raised sleeping area and lots of shredded newspaper.

The barking started immediately as we walked in. We were met by one of the volunteer kennel staff who said that a couple of the dogs were reserved, and pointed them out, other than that, all the others needed a home. We were told that some were in the paddock; others were out being walked so there may be dogs that we might miss unless we stuck around a bit.

As we walked past the doors, some of the dogs seemed to be sheltering out of the way, others were barking like crazy to get our attention. Pat, my wife, had started looking at one end; I'd started at the other and had spotted two dogs that I liked the look of.

One had already been reserved; the other was a great big brindle boy who jumped up with his paws at the bars and all his teeth showing in a great big cheesy grin. We walked up and down again but I couldn't get past Bruno, the big daft dog with the grin. There was something about him that made him stand out.

My wife wasn't so smitten.

I asked if we could take him for a walk. He was brought out of the kennel and let into the paddock whilst we were introduced to Johanna Beumer, a wonderful lady who has rehomed over five thousand greyhounds.

She told us some of Bruno's characteristics, asked about our home and family make up and concluded that Bruno was probably of the right temperament to fit in. She explained about the adoption procedure and home checks and said, 'See how you feel when you've been for a walk.'

Now complete with Bruno wearing a muzzle and lead, we set off out of the compound.

We had to stop to let a walker by with several hounds and as we did, my wife made eye contact with a large brindle bitch.

I don't know for sure what passed between them, but something did. As we started down the lane with Bruno she asked if we would be able to walk the other one that had just come back. I explained that I liked this one, she said fair enough, but she liked the one she'd just seen and wanted to see if we could walk her once we got back with Bruno.

It wasn't a problem, but I liked the big fella that was walking along so well beside me.

After several hundred yards, I stopped. It was time to turn round and head back.

Bruno had other ideas though. He head butted me in the gentleman's vegetables, and then performed the classic greyhound trick of leaving all four feet planted solidly on the ground and not budging.

A bit of fuss and some encouraging words got the big moose on the move eventually, and we headed back.

On our return, Pat asked if we could see the brindle girl that had come in from a walk.

Princess was a little less bouncy than Bruno, but was still up for another stroll.

We took the pair of them out together, and, apart from not wanting to go back to the kennels, they behaved beautifully.

We had a long chat with Johanna about the pair of them and she explained that Bruno had been injured in his last race. He suffered a broken hock and, although he was given the best of treatments and care by his trainer, he didn't recover sufficiently enough to race again and that he would probably suffer with arthritis in old age and also in the cold and damp.

Having three titanium screws holding my arthritic ankle together, I could empathise.

His trainer was covering his costs until he was rehomed.

Princess had a different story. She had raced well but, when she started to lose that little bit of pace, she was taken off the track to breed.

She'd had two litters. One of six pups and one of five.

One of the kennel maids heard that a female greyhound was going to be shot and disposed of in the afternoon and took off to go and get her. It was Princess. For reasons unknown - maybe she couldn't conceive anymore - she had outgrown her usefulness.

Bruno and Princess were housed together following that first visit of ours, and never spent a night apart over the next six years.

Three trips to the kennel for walks during the next week, a donation, completed paperwork, checks etc, and then they were in the back of the car heading to their new home.

This was the first time that I, my wife and my daughter had experienced a greyhound breaking wind....but that's another story!

Syd's Story - Julie Goddard

I'd never had a pet of my own. When I lived with my parents we had bassett hounds and they were the only breed my parents ever had. When I was about six, I went to a show with my parents and there was a Morgan Classic car - my dream car, but I doubt I will ever own one. I researched the Morgan and most of the pictures were in an art deco style. I became fascinated with the era. The more I researched, the more this gangly looking elegant hound kept showing up in the pictures, and the more I became interested in the supreme greyhound.

Many years ago, my sister lived in the Walthamstow area. We went to visit her and went to watch dog racing. A hound ran into the wall and I spent the whole evening crying. From that point I knew if I ever had a pet it would be a rescued greyhound.

Then a few years later I watched a TV programme where Annette Crosbie was talking about the plight of the greyhound. That sealed the deal for me. No other dog would ever be mine.

In 2009, my husband and I had been married for twenty-six years. We didn't have children and had never had a pet. Things changed though. Our house was burgled a few days before Christmas and life at home would never be the same in many ways for us. I went through the 2009/2010 winter dreading going home from work, knowing I would be the first one there and worrying about coming face to face with an intruder. It got to the point where I was working later and later to avoid it, I started hinting about a guard dog.

In June of 2010, I went to a boat show in Harwich and the local Retired Greyhound Trust were there. I loved the hounds and took home a brochure, which I left on the table in a prominent position. My hubby was dead set against the idea though, saying they would be a tie. Never-the-less I programmed the phone number into my mobile - well you never know!

I have twin great nephews who were going to be one-years old on 6 October 2010, and we decided in September we would travel to Ipswich to visit a well-known toy shop to buy them a pushchair bike thing that my niece wanted. We don't normally do children's shops. When we were there, I was looking at some baby alarms and some camera devices, and my husband asked me if I was really that worried about winter looming, I said yes, I was. He completely out of the blue said, 'Well we better get a dog then.' I couldn't get out of the store fast enough!

We sat in the car outside, and when I'd stopped crying, I looked up the Retired Greyhound Trust site that I'd got the brochure from and started looking for the hounds who needed rehoming. I didn't have any idea of a colour, gender or anything. The first hound that came up was this ginger looking boy called Sid. I rang the RGT there and then as we were about twenty minutes away. Unfortunately they couldn't see us right away but we made an appointment to go the next day, which was a Sunday. Elaine from RGT was really helpful and said what a great hound Sid was. He was quite small but gorgeous.

We turned up the next day at our allotted time and they brought out this gorgeous little boy hound called Sid, who, whilst he was a gorgeous brindle, wasn't the one I'd seen on the website and had dreamt about all night.

Elaine was very apologetic and said, 'Oh we had two Sid's, sorry I'll get the other one. I hope you have a big house as he's the biggest grey we've ever had.'

Within a few minutes we heard this thundering noise akin to a Great Dane rather than a greyhound, and that was the moment that Sydney Marmaduke Goddard bounded into our lives, and quite literally swept us off our feet. He owned us from that moment on.

We asked them to spell Syd with a Y as we didn't want any more confusion. Lucky for him we did have a big house.

We went and walked him for two weekends, and then on 7 October 2010, we brought him home. He still goes crazy mad when I walk in the room or if I rattle his lead, but whilst as a guard dog he's likely to kiss you to death, I cannot wait to walk through my front door spring, summer, autumn or winter, when I know he is the other side of it.

*** Editor's note - Sydney sadly died on Tuesday 20 October 2015. Have fun at the Rainbow Bridge, sweet boy x

Tommy's Story - Kerrie Vaughan

We had always had more than one dog, and when our beloved Gerrard - a lab cross - died unexpectedly, our first greyhound Chelsea changed overnight. She became a different dog in so many ways. She didn't want to eat or go for her walks; she just stayed in her bed and wouldn't interact with anyone or anything. Gerrard died a week before we went on holiday. Chelsea was going on her own holiday with my parents and their five greys, so we knew she would be okay, and hoped she would be back to her old self on our return.

How wrong we were. Once we got her home, she again went back to her bed. We then realised that she had probably never been on her own in her whole life and was grieving in the same way we were.

My husband dared to suggest getting her a companion and I told him that there was no way I could even contemplate another dog as I was totally broken hearted after losing my Gerrard.

About a week later, after seeing Chelsea look like she'd given up on life, I came round to the idea of getting her a new mate. But at the time, I was doing it for her sake as I couldn't bear to watch her go through the pain she was going through day after day.

We scoured the internet and came across the Bishops Stortford Retired Greyhound Trust, and saw a couple of potentials. My husband made a phone call and within a couple of days we met our Tommy. On that first day, we took them both out on our normal walk, and the transformation in Chelsea was amazing. Her eyes were bright as a button and her tail wouldn't stop wagging. She even did zoomies round the field, which was an absolute joy to see.

It has been just under a year since we got Tommy, and he and Chelsea are inseparable. They love each other so much and wouldn't be without each other. Even though the experience of getting Tommy at such an emotional time was hard, I have never regretted it. My life is now complete with my two greys together with my family.

William's Story - Alison Flanagan

We weren't new to greyhounds when we first encountered William. We'd had to say farewell to our first fella, Max, six months earlier. That experience had taken its toll but our second hound, Millie, had shown no signs of separation anxiety so we'd bided our time.

However, inevitably, I'd kept an eye on the website and had seen this long-overlooked, quite beautiful boy. 'A nose to make a borzoi proud,' wrote one admirer.

When one fateful Saturday morning over breakfast, my husband innocently asked, 'If we were to get a second grey, would you go for a girl or a boy?' I was ready for him.

'A boy, he's black and white and his name is William. Shall we go and have a look at him?'

Aged five, he'd been in the kennels for several years and was going stir crazy, bouncing around the walls. Whenever potential homers came to see him - he was so beautiful after all - he behaved abominably and no-one was prepared to take him on.

As 'experienced' greyhound owners, who'd already taken on challenging dogs, our interest in William was very welcome. The lane by the kennels where the hounds were walked would not really have given us adequate opportunity to get to know William, so we asked if we could take him further afield. But again we couldn't find anywhere suitable so we brought him home.

'Hmmm, I knew you wouldn't be able to resist,' said my son.

Suffice to say, William didn't go back to the kennels that day.

I'd like to be able to report it was a 'done deal', but nothing's that easy.

Saint William was his racing name but 'saint he ain't' was our initial reaction. 'Just William' described him better.

Brilliant in the house after the narrow confinement of the kennels, he also behaved well around Millie. She was a dominant girl and he was the interloper so she easily put him in his place. On walks it was a different matter. On hind legs, barking, braying, growling and snarling, he would lunge at anything on four legs in the vicinity. Muzzled and later in a harness to try to control him better, I resembled the ring master at the circus as he whirled and twirled in an effort to get closer to any other dogs who dared to trespass on his territory.

Reluctant to give up on him and condemn him to a miserable life in the kennels, I consulted friends who had experience with difficult dogs. I researched behaviourists. Nothing seemed to work. I was beginning to despair. Walks were a nightmare.

Two months on, I was still dreading the daily walks. On one of our darkest days we met up with an elderly lady. William greeted her two mannerly Labradors in his usual vociferous way. We apologised profusely, as always but she was totally unfazed.

'Don't worry,' she said, 'he'll soon calm down. Can't you see it in his eyes?' I guess some people just have that gift.

And then the seemingly impossible happened. Quite suddenly, William relaxed. All the tension left him. He would still pull enthusiastically on walks but all the aggression evaporated.

That was six years ago. Did he become the 'dream dog'? We certainly continued to have our moments! The harness was exchanged for a lead. We dared to let him off and he would return without incident. Eventually, we also released him from the muzzle. Free at last, his exuberance led him into many a scrape with nature. A thin coat and skin is a bad combination when it comes to thistles and brambles. The funniest sight was William racing into the fields in the summer. He'd bounce up and down, appearing and disappearing like Zebedee as he made his way through the tall grasses.

Anyone and everyone who frequents our local Country Park knew William. They would stop to watch in wonder and amazement as he did his stadium runs around the fields. With his cock-eyed ears and occasionally wobbly gait, he loved to greet anyone he met with a quick nuzzle around pockets in search of a treat - that long nose does come in useful - but he was equally happy with a lean and an ear rub if nothing was forthcoming.

Just a year ago he developed a lump in his neck. In September - his eleventh birthday - a biopsy confirmed an aggressive cancer. He defied the vets and our despair by continuing to live a happy life. I was hoping we'd celebrate his twelfth birthday together, but the cancer, inexorably, was taking its toll. Despite eating, he was fading away, becoming quite skeletal. When he slipped and fell he couldn't get up and would sit and wait, confused and bemused, until someone came to his rescue.

It was undignified, he deserved better than that. At home, with our long term vet and the family gathered around him, he slipped quietly away. I like to think he was grateful to us for letting him go before he deteriorated further.

The moral of William's story is that even the roughest stone can transform and polish into the brightest Kohinoor diamond.

The memory of our funny, feisty and finally grumpy old fella is etched on our hearts forever.

Merlin's Story - Jan Bebbington

After we lost Oz, our Heinz 97 dog, we had several months with just our lurcher, Megan. After debating for quite a while, we finally decided to contact the Greyhound Rescue West of England, known as GRWE for short.

So, on Saturday 11 June 2011, we set off for a kennels near Honiton to meet brother and sister hounds who'd been left tied to a post in Durham. The plan was to take Megan for a walk with the girl, as she was the more confident of the two, and see how things went. Well let's just say our Megan was not impressed. She stuck her nose in the air and ignored the poor dog completely. We then asked if we could take the boy for a walk, which went a bit better. Megan gave him a sniff and strolled up the lane with him. She'd made her mind up it was the boy or nothing!

Merlin's age and background were a mystery. We decided he was probably a town dog, as he will get in any car, hop on a bus, and walk down a busy street quite happily. He probably never lived indoors as he wasn't house trained, and the first time he went up the stairs he panicked when he turned around and realised he had to somehow get back down.

He still makes us laugh as he somehow manages to get a paw on every step when going down stairs.

Living on the edge of a town and very near green fields we thought Merlin would love it. Wrong! Hedges are scary things, water is too wet and mud gets between your toes, yuk. Four years on he will now stand in the hedge to let the tractors pass, paddle if it's really hot, but still objects to mud between his toes.

We also worried about letting him off his lead. Would he come back? What we should have worried about was, will he go anywhere? It took several weeks of my husband and me walking across the fields with a large gap between us - we looked as if we were no longer talking to each other - and encouraging Merlin to trot between us. I am pleased to say he has now worked out what to do with his long legs and will blast around the fields, still working out the braking system.

He has been nicknamed Squirely Whirley, as for the first few months his tail stayed between his legs. But slowly, as he became more confident and realised he was part of the family, the end of his tail would go around in little circles. It now makes big circles, and occasionally, if he concentrates, it will even wag properly

He still has a few issues, and will have the odd melt down, but they are getting less and less. I'm not saying it's been easy taking on a very unknown quantity, but Merlin you are very much part of the family and you do make us laugh.

Pippa and Tommy's Story - Helen Lawton

We'd looked after my friend's greyhound for the weekend and we loved the breed so much that we decided if ever we had a dog, it would have to be a grey. We couldn't have a cat as my husband is allergic to them, but he's fine with a greyhound's coat.

My husband saw a programme on TV about a dog being a child's best friend and just said, 'Let's get Holly - our daughter - a dog.'

When we told her, she cried. She'd wanted one since she was about eight-years old but we'd waited until she was ten. We decided we were going to rehome a greyhound. So, we looked on Retired Greyhound Trust Daybreaks site, and loved the look of a female hound called Pippa. But when we went over there, Ruth - who runs it - said she wasn't good with men. She'd already been rehomed once and it didn't work out for her.

My husband is nearly six-foot tall, and can look quite tough although he's a softie, so we were advised to look at other hounds in the kennels. I was called away to move my car and upon my return, Ruth greeted me at the gate, sobbing. I wondered what on earth had happened, but she just said, 'Look.'

I went into the kennels and there was my husband and my daughter, with Pippa doing the greyhound lean into my husband. She had chosen us. That was it, decision made! My husband was the only male she felt safe with as she had been badly treated by men in Ireland.

Even now, after three years with us, she only trusts the men in our family, no others.

I work in a Pupil Referral Unit, and found a fab kennels for our kids to volunteer at, walking the greyhounds. Tommy was a firm favourite as he's a gentle giant with half a tail and only four teeth. The lady who ran the kennels kept saying Pippa needed a pal, and after a few weeks we took her over to meet Tommy. A six-week fostering trial ended with Pippa having a new brother. That was over a year ago, and they get on so well, we wouldn't be without them.

Neva's Story - Charlotte Stockley

We'd had our first greyhound, Drum, for nine months when we decided to foster. We found a rescue that needed foster parents, and on 29 December 2005 we drove to Kent to collect a foster dog.

When we arrived we weren't sure which dog we would be taking, and we were offered a young blue greyhound girl or an older white and fawn girl called Neva. We decided to take Neva as we felt she had less chance of getting a home in kennels. From what we were told she'd been dumped in a shed in Ireland, with a litter of puppies, and left to fend for herself.

Sadly only four of the puppies survived. We put Neva in the car and took her home. When we got there, I took her coat off and burst into tears. She was so thin, had numerous scars, and a healing wound on her face were she had been bitten. She still managed a smile and a wag of the tail though and made herself at home.

After a few weeks, it became clear that all was not well. Neva was drinking a lot and peeing in the house. We couldn't leave her for more than about two hours without coming home to puddles on the carpet. At first we thought it was a behaviour problem, but after speaking to her rescue we decided that she needed to see a vet. She'd been to our vet on arrival and a couple of weeks later she'd been spayed, so they knew her.

Blood tests showed that her kidneys were failing. But then her blood pressure was taken and that proved to be the problem. It was nearly twice what it should have been. Our vet expressed concern and told us that she was very lucky; she could have had a stroke at any time. Thankfully, her condition could be controlled with tablets once the right dose was found. Sadly, this, combined with her age - she was five-years old - and the damage to her face, meant that no one wanted to adopt her so we said we would keep her. We had many happy years with Neva until we lost her, aged fourteen and a quarter, in July 2014.

She was the most amazing dog and touched the hearts of everyone she met. She was a wonderful Pets as Therapy dog, and used to go to events with me to promote greyhounds as pets. She was a stubborn dog who did everything on her terms including confounding our vet who'd said she would only live to about eight-years old. Neva was much loved and we really miss her.

She was my soul dog, and has left a huge paw print shaped hole in the middle of my heart.

Smelly, Jenny and Lola's Story - Amanda Jane

There was a stray cat in our garden, which we fed, and it turned out to be one of our neighbour's elderly cats. He couldn't send it to the pussycat bridge, not just yet.

We had a family meeting. Can we have a cat? No. How about a dog then? Maybe. Would we all be responsible for it? Walking, feeding etc? Yes. Okay, off to the Dogs Trust at Illfracombe we went.

We'd decided we wanted a small staffy sized girl; we ended up with a gangly eleven-month-old tan lurcher puppy.

The house check was all fine and we went and picked him up. We found out he was from a farm. He hadn't been socialized, was used for chasing for rabbits etc. But he was house trained, thankfully. He hated people waving sticks so we guess he'd been beaten. He was a lovely boy called Binx, but we named him Smelly for obvious reasons.

In August 2012, we had some guests visiting for a holiday. We'd picked up a bag of dog food for Smelly. It wasn't his usual food - for some reason we thought he might like a change of flavour. Soon after, he started scratching. We put it down to the new dog food. So, what could we do with an 18kg bag of dog kibble? Ah Woodside, one of Plymouth's Rescue centres, might like it. So we looked online - which was a mistake - to find out exactly where they were. We ended up on the rehoming page looking at the hounds who needed a home. Lots of ooh and ahh noises, and, 'Aww, look at this one.' Even our visitors were getting excited too.

We wondered would it work if we got another. We knew Smelly had had a few problems with dogs in the past, but that was in his previous life. We'd spent a lot of time and money on training classes and socialising him, so maybe he'd be better now.

We left the house and went to Cadover Bridge, one of Smelly's favourite places. After playing in the water for a while, with wet soggy feet, and a rather soggy stinky dog, we left for Woodside.

When we got there we asked if we could have a look at some of the hounds. We wandered round - more oohing and aahing - and then we saw an adorable smaller tan and white lurcher girl, called Lucy. She'd been a stray in Wales for over six months. We melted.

We went to reception and asked about her.

'Oh do you already have a dog?'

'Yes we do.'

'Oh dear. She can't be homed with another dog. She has no etiquette, no manners in the doggy world.'

The conversation turned to Smelly, the problems he'd had and how we overcame them. We must have hit a button. Was there a chance? Rather excitedly we went to the meet and free area. With both dogs muzzled, they sniffed and play bowed. We then let them off the lead.

Manic running and chasing. We couldn't believe it. Smelly came back when he was called. Under supervision their muzzles were removed. After some sniffing and licking of ears, they ran off and chased round and round up the field and back. After a while they both collapsed in a panting puddle right next to each other. Woodside couldn't believe it either. We were so pleased.

We filled out the paperwork and left.

The next day we had a phone call. They wanted to do a home check that day, which we passed, and the following afternoon we picked up our Lucy. We did think of changing her name and after a chat with our friends who were visiting, we kept it as Lucy because one of the girls was also called Lucy.

Smelly was so happy. They shared everything - sofa, toys and playtime. They even slept together.

She was only eighteen-months old when we got her. It took a year to housetrain her. She would pee in front of the door and then come and tell me. We took her to training - mixed and socialised - as much as we could.

A year and a few months later, she developed a lump right in the middle of her head. We took her to the vet for tests. She had a growth of bone about an inch on top of her head that was also growing beneath her skull. She had bone cancer. Our world fell apart. They wanted to build a fibreglass skull cap after they cut the bone away. We couldn't do that to her. She loved life, and the thought of her not being able to play in case she banged her head or fell over and knocked it was too much, so we said goodbye to her. She was our loopy, lovely, accident prone, loving friend. Her ashes are on our shelf, so she still has a home with us.

As for Smelly...Oh dear, I've never seen a dog pine before. It was heartbreaking. He wouldn't go out; he wouldn't move from the sofa, he went off his food. He was not in a good way.

He was depressed and grieving, as we all were.

We had to do something.

So, three weeks after Lucy's death we phoned Greyhound Rescue West of England and told them we would like another hound.

They did a house check, then set a date for us to visit some hounds.

We met Jenny, a gorgeous tan and brindle girl. She was a bit bossy, but just what we needed. Smelly and Jenny went for a walk together. They seemed to get on okay and had a play in the compound.

Decision time. Should we try one more just to see? As they started taking Jenny back in, she must have seen Smelly get in the car. She followed him and jumped right in. The decision was made, she chose us.

Everything was fine. Smelly got his appetite for life back, our doggy family was complete. Until around eight months later. A strange desire overcame us. Let's get another, and off we went.

We visited a few, walked with a few, and then were told a story that broke our hearts. An Irish racing girl, who been used to breed from. She'd been beaten and sold. She was kennelled with her brother, but he'd been rehomed. She'd started to shut down. No interest in life, just curled up, not caring.

We watched a video of this white and brindle spotted girl, with huge scared eyes. Afraid of men, but showing an interest in other dogs. We had to visit her. Smelly and Jenny got on well with her. But indoors, a scared, quivering girl appeared who was fearful of people, and of men talking.

But, we were sat on the floor and she put her head on my husband's lap. After a minute he stroked her ears. She tensed up, but slowly she started to relax. Her big scared eyes flinched as Mike moved his hand over her tense body; she was still scared, but allowed him to stroke her. We called her Lola.

We had a home check and they brought Lola with them. She ran through the house to the garden and had a pee. Jenny and Smelly sniffed her. As soon as we moved, she ran further up the garden, afraid of us. Would this work? We had to try.

46

We brought Lola indoors with the other two dogs and that was the start of a two-week home trial, which ended with us keeping her. It's been tough, but with patience and love, those scared, caught in the headlights eyes are changing. She leans into you for cuddles; she's learning to be cheeky. She barks at feeding time, just in case we forget.

And we believe it was meant to be that we had the girls, because whilst checking the history of our greyhounds, we discovered that they had the same great, great grandfather.

It's been nearly a year since we got Lola...and now we're thinking of fostering!

Nugget's Story - Lin Lenox

I never thought I would have a greyhound. I've always loved dogs - growing up I was never without one. When I married and had children of my own I bought a rough collie called Crystal - after Crystal Gail, because of the long hair.

When she was two I bred from her, and she produced six female puppies. Of course we had to keep one, who we called Gemma.

After losing both of them, I bought a sheltie - Hollie - who in later years was unable to walk far. As we loved walking, my husband Rob and I decided to travel from Romford to Maldon on as many Sundays as possible, to walk the greyhounds from Clark's kennels.

I was really surprised to see what gentle animals they were and we used to walk four at a time, up to twenty in a morning.

I'd already decided that any future dogs would be rescues, but thought a greyhound might be possible. It would depend on Hollie being happy to share her home with one, of course.

We first saw Nugget on the Brentwood Greyhound Rescue website. She was only eighteen-months old and looked beautiful.

We went to see her and couldn't believe she hadn't been snapped up. It seemed that nobody liked her overshot jaw. We decided she was the one for us and took Hollie to meet her. All went well.

We then took them both to a local park, where Nugget went straight into a pond - she obviously didn't recognise a stretch of water. She then knocked over my coffee and proceeded to lap it up with Hollie's help. That was the start of her love for lattes!

We'd already sold our house, and were moving to the Isle of Wight a week later, but were still allowed to collect Nugget. I had to drive over on my own as Rob had a job interview but the two dogs were fine in the car, Nugget used Hollie as a fluffy pillow!

Nugget gave Hollie a new lease of life and it was wonderful to see the friendship build up between them.

Unfortunately we lost Hollie within a year. But Nugget was a godsend then as she kept me busy with her training.

I was told that greyhounds would not learn tricks - wrong!
Nugget soon learned to sit, speak, give paws, bow, roach on

command of 'greyhound,' circle me both ways, weave between my legs, and hi-five.

She runs off lead and will stop on command even if she sees a cat. She does lick her lips though!

I recommend greyhounds to everyone we meet as they are such wonderful companions.

Bryn's Story - Claire Standen

After a lot of thought and discussion with each other and the Kent Greyhound Rescue, my husband and I decided that a greyhound may be for us. We were invited to the kennels to have a look at the hounds.

On 11 May 2013, off we went, still not sure, and a bit apprehensive. We were made very welcome, and several hounds were bought out to meet us.

They didn't seem to be interested in us until Bryn appeared. He was led over to us very slowly with his tail and head down and he looked so sad. Bryn walked around us then stopped in front of me, leant against me and put his head in my hand.

Well that was that, he was mine, no more discussion, decision made!

The next week was spent having a house check and buying beds, bowls, toys etc. Everything we thought he'd need.

On the 18th we went to collect Bryn. He'd only been fostered for three hours as he refused to walk on laminate flooring, and wasn't house trained. He was also absolutely petrified.

I could have cried he was so sad. When we got home, the kitchen floor was a real problem, so we put down carpet tiles, useful for taking up and washing while house training!

Slowly Bryn settled, and over the last two years he has become braver, cheekier and funnier, and he loves people. He has learnt to sit, give a paw and go down; his recall is excellent - but only for me. He doesn't understand the point of toys, but he loves TV remotes, mobile phones and door wedges!   His favourite treat is ice cream.

Our lovely boy has won several rosettes, including best greyhound, and some best in shows.

We love him so much, and are really proud of him. Everyone needs a greyhound in their lives.

Charlie's Story - Sally Hill

My first greyhound was called Charlie. He was a large fawn and white dog. At the time I was running my business - The Animal Nursing Home - in Sussex, and Charlie came in as a patient having been involved in a road accident.

Despite many attempts with the vets to stimulate his front leg to work again, it proved unsuccessful. It just dangled there and was useless to him. So, the decision was jointly made to amputate it.

His owners came to visit a couple of times and Charlie was so brave throughout all the recovery period. Then his owners contacted me and said they didn't want him back as he didn't suit their lifestyle with only three legs.

So poor Charlie was unwanted, despite all the trauma he'd endured.

I decided to adopt him and he remained with me for the rest of his days.

I heard that his previous owners had subsequently gone out and bought a cocker spaniel puppy!

Sadly at the age of nine, about six years later, Charlie succumbed to cancer and I lost him. He was the most lovely, brave and affectionate dog, and he was the first of many greyhounds, and the start of my involvement in greyhound and lurcher rescue, which I still continue to this day.

Luna's Story - Sharon Fane

We'd lost our rescued, Shih Tzu, Gizzie, at the grand old age of eighteen and were without a dog for eighteen months. Around this time my husband and I got talking to a man who walked his greyhound in the woods. His dog just leaned on me and calmly stayed there whilst I fussed him for many minutes. That dog began to cast the greyhound spell over me. After that, every time I saw a person walking a greyhound, I would stop and talk to them about their dog.

I was told time and time again how amazing greys are as pets, and every time I petted their hounds I was rewarded with a lean and such calm, gentleness that I needed to know more. When I was out shopping one day, I noticed a flier advertising our local retired greyhound kennels, so my husband and I volunteered as walkers. We walked about eight retired hounds each week for eight months. We fell in love many times, especially with a blue hound called Lenny and a black boy called Mannie.

When they were both rehomed I felt a little break in my heart, but a huge relief that they were going to start new, happier lives.

One Saturday morning in October 2012, we turned up to walk the hounds and the kennel owner said, 'I have a dog for you.'

She had come in on Thursday night and the owner had reserved her straight away for us. He brought this thin, scared, blue hound out for us to walk. She was frightened of absolutely everything, and stood shaking and panting in front of us, but we looked into her eyes and knew she was going to be ours.

We had a home check and passed it, Luna came to visit, and luckily for us, took one look at our cats, turned away and went and hid in the corner.

Just over a week later, on 27 October, Luna came home, her Gotcha Day.

Unfortunately, she'd been attacked in kennels by another dog and had open wounds and stitches. She was also very nervous. She stayed under the radiator in our living room for two months. We had to slip the lead on her to take her in to the garden. Then one night in December, she got out from under the radiator, laid by my feet and she's been there ever since.

Those first few months she needed a lot of care and understanding as she'd been badly bitten. I washed her wounds and brushed her gently, stroking and talking to her as much as I could.

We also gave her plenty of space to just lie, watching us and sussing us out. It turned out she had been tried for racing - twice - but she wouldn't chase the hare and only ran along to play with the other hounds. She was unwanted at just twenty-two months. Their loss, and what a fantastic gain for us!

We now have a beautiful, happy, wonderful girl who we both adore. She has been on holidays with us, and out to dinner, but is always amazingly well behaved.

We've made many friends in greyhound Facebook groups, and on the retired greyhound monthly walks. We have a whole new social life because of Luna. We couldn't imagine life without her.

*** Editor's note - sadly, since Sharon wrote this story, Luna has died. Run free at the Bridge, sweetheart.

Nutty's Story - Trudie Scott

We'd always had dogs - usually ones that no one wanted - but as the children grew up and I was working longer hours, it didn't seem fair to leave a dog at home on its own for most of the day.

Then I stopped working for what I thought at the time, was the rest of my life, so I pestered my other half to get a dog.

We weren't fans of small breeds and I wasn't able to spend hours striding across the hills with an energetic dog, so we pondered for a while about a greyhound. Eventually I spoke to Kent Greyhound Rescue and told them how I spent my day and asked if that kind of lifestyle would suit a greyhound. The reply was, 'They'd think they've died and gone to heaven.'

So, a greyhound it was going to be; or was it? Having only ever met two greyhounds my entire life - both of which were black - I thought a trip to the kennels just to see if they were really a breed I wanted, would be a good idea. In my mind I imagined a sleek black boy.

I took a friend with me as I thought I might be able to see a couple of dogs, and it would be good to have someone to talk over the relative merits of the breed, and the individual dogs. The plan was to visit the kennels again in a couple of months ready for the warmer weather with my other half, to find a dog together.

So, my friend and I arrived, and the kennel maid brought out Nutty. He was a large, mainly white, fluffy greyhound who was smothered in speckles of every colour from pale golden to black, with two brindle splodges on his head. My friend was, as the saying goes 'all over him like a rash.'

Nutty seemed very quiet and I just gently made a fuss of him. With my friend on my right side, Nutty chose to stand on my left leaning against me. Though he had a really thick kennel coat, it was obvious even to the untrained eye that he was underweight and traumatised.

He had a cut on his nose, the tips of both ears had scabs on them, and behind both ears where his collar rubbed there were sores the size of a fifty-pence piece. He also had a lump on his elbow, an injury he'd sustained when they were loading him in Ireland.

It was a cold but bright February day and I could see the sun shining through the skin on his legs, and though it sounds soppy, I just felt my heart melt.

The longer we stood there, the more he leaned against me. I don't quite know what happened to the black greyhound I was going to get, but there was no way I wasn't going to give this dog a home.

I was able to arrange a home check for the next day, Friday. Because I wanted Nutty to have part of the day with us before bed time, we arranged to collect him on Sunday, but by Saturday afternoon I was free, so I rang and arranged to collect him then. By the time we got home it was almost dark and finally my other half got to meet his best buddy. Like me, he fell instantly in love with this rather scared greyhound.

It wasn't always plain sailing for the first few months, and nine months later Nutty became very ill. We almost lost him three times, but I'm delighted to say that several operations and a couple of dozen vet bills later, he is fit and healthy, and such a joy that we just had to have another. I wouldn't ever want to be without 'our boys.'

Purdey's Story - Sharon Pinder

My dad was diagnosed with cancer in April 2008, and at the time he had a black greyhound called Skye. In August of 2008, he had his first major operation to remove the cancer and hopefully give him some more time with us.

Sadly, at the end of April 2010, his beloved Skye was put to sleep through old age. After less than a week, he realised he needed the love of another greyhound to give him the strength and a reason to go on fighting this terrible disease. He was on his own, and struggling with a quiet, empty house and no dog to walk. It was the dog that had made him get up every morning and gave him people at his local park to socialize with.

He asked me if I'd help him find a rescue centre, so my internet search began. I spoke to a centre in Cornwall, but they weren't very accommodating. My next port of call was to a lovely, enthusiastic lady called Vicky Gregory at the Retired Greyhound Trust Hillview in Honiton. We fully explained my dad's condition, but it didn't worry her in the least; in fact she suggested we come to the centre at our earliest opportunity.

We took him there the following weekend so he could meet Vicky and the dogs. We spent hours walking various dogs, all of whom he would have happily rehomed. But he decided he wanted the one who needed to be rehomed the most, and who had been at the centre the longest, which was Ally.

She had barely any teeth, scars all over her body, and numerous bald patches, but the most gorgeous eyes imaginable. It was love at first whinge...Ally does this constantly!

Just as we were getting ready to leave, and whilst Dad was completing his paperwork, Paul - Vicky's husband - brought out another greyhound that they had to keep in their house as all the kennels were full, for a toilet break.

Can I just say at this point my husband Brian and I had no intention of getting a dog, this visit was purely for my dad, however the above mentioned dog, who was called Purdey, came straight over, snuck in between us and laid her head on our legs. We were smitten; it was love at first cuddle

We asked if we could walk her, to give us the chance to discuss things, and couldn't ignore the feeling that she had just chosen us and it was meant to be.

We returned to Vicky full of smiles, and asked hopefully if we could offer her a loving home.

We were told she'd only been there a week after being found abandoned, alone, and hungry in a car park, where it transpired she had been for over a month.

Vicky very kindly offered to drive Ally down to my dad's without a home check as he had had many greyhounds previously; therefore she was confident he was a suitable prospective owner. She also said she would come and do a home check on us at the same time.

Thankfully we passed with flying colours, and a week later went back to Honiton to collect our beautiful girl.

Since then, I've become the home checker for Vicky in Plymouth and all surrounding areas. Purdey has accompanied me on all my checks, including to the home of Cherry, the dog in the first story.

Sadly after a six-year battle, I lost my dad in 2014, but Ally is now happily seeing out her last few years with my sister and her cats.

Purdey is my baby and my life, and along with my wonderful husband Brian, has helped me through the last few difficult months since losing my dad. Her unconditional love and devotion gets me through the days.

She has proven to be the most fantastic greyhound, with great recall. She is never on a lead whilst out on a walk, and has been so loving and gentle – and most patient at times - growing up with our four-year-old granddaughter.

We really couldn't have asked for more.

Hugo and Portia's Story - Julia Deacon

In 2006, we visited the Retired Greyhound Trust in Brighton as I'd heard that greyhounds were in need of homes and what wonderful pets they made.

So we were there looking at the dogs, and this beautiful big boy came straight over and leaned on first me, then my husband.

It was love at first sight.

The dog's name was Hugo, his racing name was Reyes. He was only three-years old. He'd raced all over the country and apparently was very fast, but was retired due to having sore wrists.

The home check was done, which we passed, and we collected him soon after.

It felt as if we'd always had him. He was so good and was a real mummy's boy.

Unfortunately, later on, his racing injuries surfaced and he was quite poorly for the last few years of his life.

About three months after getting Hugo, we went to a greyhound day - just to have a look you understand – and saw a lovely girl called Portia. Her racing name was Glendale Maid. She'd been brought over from Ireland with four of her siblings. They were all were due to be put to sleep until Celia Cross at Sun Valley kennels stepped in and rescued them.

At this point we hadn't decided on another greyhound, but Hugo loved her, so that was that.

Unfortunately she came with a lot of problems. She didn't like to be touched, and the poor girl was covered in scars, which looked like cigarette burns.

But with love and patience, her very cheeky character came out. She was quite naughty and rather aloof. Hugo adored her and followed her everywhere so we now had double trouble!

Over the years she's mellowed. She's still not keen on cuddles, but loves being stroked and brushed and loves giving kisses. She's very sweet natured, although she can still be rather aloof at times.

Sadly, we lost our boy Hugo recently, but one day we will have another greyhound. Owning ours has opened our eyes as to how many are retired and in need of homes. They are such a beautiful and gentle breed, I'd recommend them to everyone.

Solar's Story - Sheena Clarke

I'd had to let my German shepherd go to the Rainbow Bridge just short of his thirteenth birthday. I'd rescued him as a young dog, and he'd had a good life. Getting another dog had been on my mind, but I'd felt in no rush. My friend Holly, at the stables where my horse was kept, felt I needed another dog in my life and often dropped hints from time to time.

One day, Holly called round to tell me there was an advert in the pet shop window down in Rickmansworth, that read, 'Retired racing greyhounds, looking for good homes.'

'Let's give the trainer a ring and go and see them,' she'd said.

'Well, I'm not sure a greyhound is for me,' I'd replied. I tried to picture a greyhound in my mind. Ah yes, thin stick dog, with kind eyes. I thought back to a small box amongst the 'Dogs for Sale' column in the Horse and Hound in the early nineties. It'd had a picture of a greyhound and underneath it had said, 'Greyhounds make loving pets.'

The only time I remember actually meeting a greyhound, was a resident one at the local stables. He was a large fawn lad and was very friendly. On cold winter evenings, we would gather in the barn he would come in and lie on the straw bales with his head on our laps, soaking up all the fuss, which appeared to come in an endless supply for him.

So I said to Holly, 'I guess there is no harm in looking,' and before I could finish my sentence, arrangements had been made to meet a greyhound at the trainer's house later that day. We were shown into the front room, and there in the corner stood a little black greyhound girl called Solar, who had loads of pretty white dots in her coat. She was very shy and had a distant look in her eye.

It would be great to say it was love at first sight, but if I am honest, all I could see was a really underweight dog with very little personality. We took her a little way down the road and she walked beside me, not looking about or sniffing. I took her back and was asked would I be taking her home there and then? I needed to think and said I would let them know.

Again if I am honest, my thoughts were probably, is this really the dog for me?

We left, and for the next few days I thought about her on and off. However, by Saturday I couldn't get her out of my mind and felt sad leaving her in the kennels. I knew there was a vulnerability attached to this girl, and maybe I could be the one to help her.

I talked it over that afternoon with a good friend, Mike, and the next thing, I was calling the trainer's wife to ask if the dog was still looking for a home.

Yes she was.

The weather was unseasonably cold, it was the 16 June 2001, around two in the afternoon, and it had rained all day, steady and heavy, the sort that just doesn't give up and gets you soaked very quickly.

Mike and I pulled into the kennels, and standing in a gravel car park was the trainer and next to him was Solar, looking very bedraggled.

We climbed out of the car and the trainer brought her over. He had a slightly impatient look on his face and I was mindful of his wife's words from half an hour earlier. I knew he'd be leaving soon with a car load of greyhounds heading for Reading Greyhound Stadium for the Saturday race night.

'Here she is,' he said. Pointing to a very old tatty collar and lead he added, 'you can borrow these, till you get your own.'

I took hold of the lead and Solar, who seemed more concerned about the inclement weather than realising what a momentous occasion this was and that her life was about to change forever.

He also handed me an enormous dirty and stained white plastic muzzle with instructions that this must be worn when she was out in public.

With little else to say, I led her round to get into the car. The trainer gave her a parting pat, wished us well and walked quickly away without a backward glance. It felt like I had just picked up an old racing bike, which was of no use to its previous owner, and with it gone, there would be more space for something better.

Solar stood in the back of my friends four by four, looking slightly shell-shocked. All previous thoughts of the bad weather were gone, her main concern had switched to the more pressing situation she'd found herself in, and by the look on her face this was not the favourable choice. We pulled slowly out onto the lane and

Solar kept standing, I would like to say it was for enjoyment, but it looked like anything but, and she had to work hard to keep her balance - leaning and swaying with the movement of the car. Sometimes, she didn't quite judge it right and ending up tottering backwards, forwards and sideways. Her dark eyes were wide and wild, and despite the cold day, she was panting hard. I watched her from my seat and thought, what have I done, have I made a huge mistake in taking this dog home?

Within an hour she was in my house and officially my dog, although no paper work or money had crossed hands. It would be lovely to say we started to bond straight away, but this was not the case, and for the first month, I walked and fed her, but still wondered if we were right for each other. She probably felt exactly the same, if only she could have said.

Needless to say, that did all change, but as much as I would like to take credit for this, the help actually came in the form of another greyhound.

His name was Foss, a large, handsome, confident, Dunn brindle, and he'd coincidently come from the same racing kennels as Solar. In the kennels Solar was known as Saigon Mist and they'd been kennelled together.

By some twist of fate, Foss had been homed a month earlier and was living in the same village. After meeting up again, Solar blossomed, whatever Foss did Solar copied, having carried her up and down my steep stairs for weeks, Foss came round and she bounded up the stairs after him as if she had done it all her life.

Suddenly, people were her long lost friends and instead of hiding behind my legs or in another room, she would be out in front, jostling for position and leaping up and down. With her new found confidence, this little girl lived life to the full. She was excellent off the lead, one call from me and she would turn on a sixpence back to my side. She loved to come out when I rode my horse, running along beside us, her long tail waving in all directions with excitement. She played with every friendly dog in the park, no matter how big or small.

She was clever too. Able to sit and go down, she could fetch, and easily achieved her Bronze and Silver Good Citizen awards. She also won best in shows and even came second at Crufts.

I loved her smile and her gentle nature, but best of all was our bond. An inseparable bond that made my heart burst with pride, joy and love.

I looked back and thought, how could I have misjudged this girl so much on that wet day in June 2001? Solar packed a lot into the six years she was with me. Sadly her life was taken too early. Just short of her tenth birthday she succumbed to kidney disease. I shall always be indebted to Solar for introducing me to the wonderful world of greyhounds, and of course I knew I would have to open my heart to another - even though I was heartbroken at Solar's loss - so along came Lilly. However, that is another story.

Bandit's Story - Marie Dillon

Gary and I had been together for a couple of years, when we decided that we'd like a dog for some company during our walks in the Kent countryside.

The only problem was that we couldn't agree on what sort, he'd had greyhounds previously and I had always had Heinz 57s. We both agreed though that it would be a rescue dog.

We searched websites but still couldn't decide on a breed.

Gary then found the greyhound rescue site for Harvel, and said, 'They need people to walk the dogs, shall we give it a go?'

I - in my ignorance - said, 'If you like, but I'm not having an ugly dog like those.'

A view that my children shared and voiced frequently whenever the subject of dogs was discussed.

We went along to Harvel and were offered four dogs to walk, but they all had to be muzzled. I was horrified as Gary had told me they were gentle dogs so why did they need muzzles? After having the reasons explained, we walked the dogs round the village green and up through the woods. It was lovely. One of the dogs seemed quite sweet, but he was very aloof.

The following weekend we were back at Harvel, and we were given another four dogs, and the aloof boy was there again. He walked so beautifully beside me, stopping when asked and not pulling at all, whilst the others were all over the place trying to get close. As we stopped on the green and sat on a bench for a stroke and a cuddle with the dogs, Mr Aloof came alongside and tried to rub his muzzle off.

In the thirty seconds that it took me to hold his face and say that I couldn't take it off, just in case anything happened, I fell in love. He'd looked at me with his soft brown eyes and that was it. I was his. Gary didn't come into the equation, I had found my boy - even though I wasn't looking for a greyhound - and nothing was going to stop me from taking him home.

After taking all of five minutes to persuade Gary that Mr Aloof - who was actually called Bandit - was the dog that I wanted, and it seemed that he wanted me, we arranged to get a home check done.

The day couldn't come soon enough. After a couple of

recommendations such as putting tape on the conservatory doors to stop him running into them, and raising the fence on one side of the back garden, we were given the all clear to collect Bandit.

We checked his racing record - his name had been Lena's Bandit - and we were glad to see he hadn't retired with an injury.

We collected Bandit the following weekend. He was so excited to be in the car, not nervous like I'd expected. Once at home however, he became very nervous.

We found an old quilt and put it in the corner of the living room next to the settee for him to lie on. For the next few days, we actually had to put him on a lead to take him outside into the back garden for the toilet, and everything else. After, he always ran back to the quilt in his corner - which coincidentally was next to where I sat - for safety.

Eventually he got used to his routine, and started to enjoy his walks along the river, stopping for a paddle and a drink.

It wasn't long before we were able to let him off lead wherever we walked. Once he'd had a zoomie session to burn of his excess energy, he always stayed right behind me.

During one of his first off lead episodes, Bandit was running between both of us and getting treats and cuddles for coming back. In his excitement, and travelling at a very fast speed towards Gary, he swerved at the last minute as usual to avoid running into him. Unfortunately Gary also moved to avoid the collision. Result? Gary completely upended and on his backside, Bandit looking totally confused, and me unable to speak I was laughing so much.

Bandit became everybody's favourite dog, winning us all over with his gentle ways and silly behaviour, which of course he stopped as soon as he thought we were laughing at him or trying to take a photo. Our friends started wanting to go for walks with us and our beloved hound. They soon came to love him as much as we did, and a couple of them rescued their own dogs – though not greyhounds unfortunately.

On many occasions he joined us in our local pub, and became the first dog that one of our nervous friends stroked because of his calming manner.

Bandit had my heart and I had his. He slept next to me on the settee, which we bought from eBay especially for him, on the floor, and in the bedroom. My sons nicknamed him the Old Sop and

Mummy's Boy because he was always with me.

He changed our lives and I hope that we changed his. He only had to look at me with his big brown eyes and I said yes to whatever he wanted!

We still walked the dogs in the kennels whenever we could, and Bandit never minded sharing us for those short periods, but he always had a grin on his face when he climbed back in the car to come home again.

After a couple of years with just Bandit, whilst walking at the kennels one day we were shown a little girl called Betty who had a receding bottom jaw and was very underweight. She was pining because she'd been put back into kennels after her owner's circumstances had changed. Bandit adopted her too, but she is a whole other story!

We had Bandit for nearly six very happy years, and took him everywhere with us until the dreaded cancer took him from us. It absolutely broke all of our hearts and we still think that he's around when we get strange things happening in the house. Betty missed him and pined dreadfully, they'd been our bookends for over four years, mirroring each other on opposite ends of the settee.

He changed all of our lives with his gentle nature, and completely changed mine and my children's perception of greyhounds. We all still miss him and there isn't a day that passes without us thinking about him.

We feel that he sent our lurcher, Macca, to us as he knew that Macca needed special love to get him through his short life - he was epileptic.

Don't let anyone tell you that greyhounds are ugly dogs, they are beautiful, both inside and out.

Prince's Story - Gary Dillon.

Back in the early eighties I got my first greyhound. I'd just purchased my first house, and after a few months of living alone, I thought it would be nice to have a canine companion to welcome me home every day.

I did some research and thought a retired greyhound would be the ideal dog.

I was chosen by Prince a lovely four-year-old fawn dog from a rescue centre in Surrey.

He settled in really well and became a huge part of my life, and whenever I was at work I arranged for my neighbours to call in and let him out during the day.

We used to love going for long walks, especially at weekends when we could walk for miles. He was getting used to being off the lead and coming straight back to me for strokes and cuddles. Perfect.

Then one evening we were sitting watching the TV, cuddled up on the settee, when the phone rang.

'Is that Mr Dillon?'

'Yes,' I replied, 'who is this?'

'This is the RSPCA,' came the answer.

Slightly concerned I asked if there was a problem.

'We've had a report that the dog you own is being mistreated.'

I was, to say the least, a bit upset by the statement.

'Who's told you that? What are you talking about?' I wanted to know.

'We can't tell you that, but one of our officers called by this afternoon and no one was at home.'

I tried to explain that I was at work and that the neighbour calls in to let Prince out.

'That may be so, Mr Dillon, but there is also evidence that your dog is under-nourished.'

I couldn't believe what the man was saying, and I proceeded to tell him exactly what Prince was being fed daily and even what treats I gave him.

'Well our officer managed to look through your living room window and has told us he looks extremely thin for his size.'

That was it I could no longer control myself.

70

'It's a bloody greyhound. They are bred like that. I cannot believe that the RSPCA of all people have called me for this!'

'Well we would like to arrange a visit so we can see for ourselves that you are looking after him properly.'

Once again I informed the caller, 'IT'S A BLOODY GREYHOUND, THEY ARE ALL LIKE THAT.'

It was then that I could hear the laughter and giggling in the background, as my mate came clean, and I realised it was a hoax call, and in his words, 'he had done me up like a kipper.'

To this day whenever I see him with our latest grey addition, he will comment on how thin it is and am I feeding it correctly? It's a greyhound you know, they are special.

Bonny's Story – Valerie Potts

It was nearly twenty years ago now, but I was going through a really rough time. I lost my mum in the May, and then lost my husband the following January. In between I'd broken my leg really badly and had to have it pinned and plated.

My dad was struggling with being alone and so was I, so my sister-in-law and I decided to take dad to the Blue Cross to look for a cat to keep him company. We'd always had cats while I was growing up.

I decided not to walk round the cattery, but on my own I went to walk round the kennels. There was a lot of noise from barking dogs in the first block. In the second block there was the same noise but half way along it went quiet and a long legged black dog was just standing there looking out. She was called Beth. Slowly she came over, jumped up and put her nose through the bars at me. She seemed to know that I was sad.

A week later, she came home. Beth became Bonny,

I had no idea what breed of dog she was. I knew that she'd been thrown out of a car on the A33 Winchester bypass, and that she'd sustained a broken toe and a few cuts.

She kept me going. She got me up in the morning and I made new friends while walking her.

She wasn't a very easy dog initially. In those early days she took no notice of me and was rather naughty. She'd do things like run and roll around in manure, and one day, I'd been out shopping, and I got home to find she had taken my big plant out of the pot, and had run from one sofa to the other, back and forth, so there was soil everywhere.

I phoned my sister-in-law and just sat and cried. We cleaned it up, and from that day Bonny and I seem to have an understanding. She settled down into a wonderful companion, and I grew to adore that dog.

I may have saved her, but she also saved me, from a very lonely, sad existence.

Since then, I've had and lost three more greyhounds, but I now have five. They are wonderful dogs and make fantastic pets.

Fleur's Story - Katie Piggott

I'd been working as a volunteer for the Retired Greyhound Trust for about six months at two separate kennels. My love for the greyhound breed grew by the second, as the more I met, the more transfixed I became.

I owned a Maine coon cat called Jobe, who was nineteen-years young, and a blind border collie called Mabel, but I dreamed of owning my own retired greyhound when Jobe died.

One day I got a call to do a home check for a local couple who were adopting a timid three-year-old bitch greyhound from Essex, called Blue.

I met the charming couple, who admitted they were completely green on the subject of retired greyhound protocol, but they had a lovely home. They passed the home check, and eager to get things right, they told me all about this cat friendly blue greyhound who they were going to call Darcy. She'd been homed before, but had been returned a few times.

I left my contact number with them in case they had any problems, and when I left, I don't know why but I felt a bit uneasy about the whole thing.

It wasn't long before I received a call.

I drove over to them imagining all sorts of things...

When I arrived, this beautiful, timid, petrified greyhound girl was in total shut down.

Unable to make eye contact, and unable to move, it took forty minutes to get her to take a treat from me.

I crawled around on the floor in submit pose, and she eventually, but reluctantly, made eye contact.

The couple couldn't keep her. It wasn't their fault; the poor hound was just too shut down and troubled for them to deal with.

So, even though I had a cat, I took her home. If I didn't try to help this poor girl, I didn't think anyone else would. I called her Fleur, because she was like a beautiful flower, just waiting to blossom. Mabel the border collie accepted her immediately.

It has been a long road, but every problem that cropped up, I met head on, and with lots of helpful advice we got there. I took things gently, making sure I went at Fleur's pace.

She spent most of her time in her crate, which was her 'safe place.'

She was a bit underweight, was very scared of males, children, loud noises, and traffic.

Her background is a bit shady. She was a non racer and had two failed rehomings at the young age of one, and two-years old.

Initially, her fears seemed to be getting worse, but, nine months on, she is a dear, wonderful dog to have around.

She will never be a massive personality, she's too timid and wary for that, but what she lacks in personality she makes up for in beauty and with lots of love and patience, her fears are getting under control.

She has become quite the little show greyhound too. She loves the show ring. So far, she's won several first prizes, and Reserve and Best in Show awards at various dog shows. It's such an achievement for a dog that was completely shut down when I first saw her.

I went on to adopt another greyhound, Fin, aged three, and a saluki, Farah, aged fifteen months. Mabel the blind border collie is seven.

So my pack now consists of four dogs and that's my limit...for now!

Darling Fleur is flourishing in her family environment, I'm so incredibly proud of her and her journey so far.

She is the sweetest greyhound, with her beautiful soulful expression.

Whatever happened to her in the past may still be giving her painful memories, but hopefully they will fade in time. That's my aim for her, and I have all the time in the world.

Bess's Story – Kate Densham

I've always wanted a greyhound. Every time I was asked while growing up, 'What dog would you have?' or, 'what's your favourite breed of dog?' Always, straight away without hesitation, I'd say, 'A greyhound.'

In my twenties we had cats, and I owned a horse. I met a lady called Ann Raynor because we kept our horses at the same yard. She had lurchers, and then she got a greyhound from a greyhound sanctuary called Russets. It was a local place I wasn't aware of, even though I only lived about five miles away from it.

I was so envious, but I couldn't have a dog yet as I still lived with my parents, so it got pushed to the back of my mind.

A few years later, I sold my horse, met my other half, Ross, and moved into a bungalow. But we were renting and still couldn't have a dog.

We regularly went on long country walks, or down to the beach, and it just felt wrong without a dog, like something was missing.

We often talked about getting dogs, and Ross warmed to the greyhound idea. We longed to move into our own house so we could explore the possibility.

Four years on, I found the ideal house. We put in an offer and started the ball rolling. We hoped for a swift transaction as there was no chain on either side, so I friended Russet Sanctuary's Facebook page, and noticed they were having an open day in August.

We jumped at the chance to go and have a chat with people and show our interest. The idea was that we'd move into the new house and have a bit of time to sort it out before looking for our fur baby.

At the open day we chatted to lots of nice people, and when we were on our way to the kennels, we were met by a black female hound called Bess, who wore a bib saying, 'I need a home.'

She was enjoying the fuss and attention we gave her and seemed quite relaxed while we chatted to Nic and Sue who were fostering her with their other hounds and a collie. They told us all about Bess and she sounded ideal for us. They'd have liked to keep her, but it just wasn't the right time for them.

We carried on walking around while watching Bess. Other

people showed her attention, but she was a bit jumpy and unsettled with them. Before we left, we went and said goodbye to her. I thought about her all the way home and for days after, but I didn't want to get my hopes up in case someone else rehomed her.

I told Ann all about her, and she said she knew Nic and Sue, so we all started chatting on Facebook.

They suggested that we reserve Bess, as she'd only been happy when having a fuss from us, so I called Sandra at the sanctuary, and she told us to come up and meet Bess again with no distractions.

She was concerned because people had been visiting the kennels but Bess wouldn't go near them.

When we got there, I said to Ross, 'If she doesn't like us then that's ok, when we're settled in the new house, we can come again.'

As we stood waiting for Bess to come out we were worried that she'd cower away, but no, she ran straight up to us! Sandra was so pleased, as were we, so we reserved Bess, praying that we'd be moving in to the new house soon.

I cried when I got home, the bond between us was already there.

Then there were delays with the house. The vendors had problems with the house they were buying and I had to keep calling Sandra to keep her in the loop. I was so afraid we would lose Bess. But, although it was a lot later than planned, we finally moved in on Halloween.

One week later, we collected Bess and took her home.

It's been nearly a year since we met her and she's settled in so well. We hate being apart from her. Our love for her grows stronger each day. She changes every week, and little quirks come out in her character all the time. We take her on a greyhound walk every month, and we're taking her to the open day as part of the family. You never know, maybe we will be chosen by another greyhound.

Poppy Jones' Story – Jean Armstrong

When our rough Collie died in 1996, I was dogless for the first time in nearly forty years. I considered getting a Bernese mountain dog puppy, but before this came to fruition, family circumstances led to us 'inheriting' a young brindle whippet cross lurcher called Bertie. He turned out to be the sweetest dog you could meet and got us into hounds.

One day my daughter said, 'Why don't we get Bertie a friend? 'and suggested an ex racing greyhound. I wasn't that keen, my only association with greyhounds up until then had been my mother exclaiming, 'Oh my God, Fred Harris has just gone down with his greyhounds, get the cat in!'

Also, I'd always preferred long-haired breeds, greyhounds seemed so skinny and sharp looking, and I enjoyed having my dogs off lead and playing Frisbee or ball with them. I knew that most people had to keep greyhounds on leads in public places, and wasn't sure how I felt about keeping a dog on a lead most of the time.

However my daughter kept on about a greyhound, so eventually I phoned Wimbledon Greyhound Welfare to ask if they had any potentially cat friendly dogs for adoption. The lady said they had had one, but it had been rehomed a few days before, and there was nothing else at the moment. She took my details and said she would call me if another became available.

Four or five days later, I had a call to say the bitch they had rehomed previously had been returned to the kennels, and were we interested in going to see her?

We arranged to see her later that week, which happened to coincide with my daughter's birthday, so on the day we made the one hundred mile round trip to the WGW kennels in Godstone, Surrey.

On arrival we were taken to a wire fenced area, where a pretty blue brindle greyhound came running towards us, pressed her nose up against the wire and licked my hand. She was then led out of the run to meet Bertie, who she immediately growled at and turned her attention back to me. I remember saying to her, 'It's no good you liking just me, if you don't like Bertie, you can't come home with us.'

She seemed to understand and treated him with indifference

80

for the rest of the meeting. It looked as though they were going to be okay so we decided to adopt Poppy Jones as she was called, and were allowed to take her home that afternoon.

Poppy was termed a non-chaser and had retired from racing at nineteen-months old, but we were the third home she'd had. The first was with a woman who had a mentally disturbed son who tried to attack Poppy with an axe, so she was removed from there pretty quickly. The next was with a gay couple who adored her, but unfortunately their cats didn't. One refused to go downstairs, and the other attacked Poppy at every opportunity. Reluctantly they decided to return her to the kennels, so it was the third time lucky with us.

Poppy settled in well. Initially we kept her muzzled because of our three cats, but it wasn't long before she was able to keep the muzzle off when we were at home, and only wear it when she was left on her own with them.

When we'd had Poppy for three months, WGW held a show at Epsom racecourse, which we thought we should support. My daughter, Poppy and I set off on a damp overcast Sunday in July 1998. I remember it well because we got a puncture on the M25 and started trying to change the wheel when a kind motorway maintenance worker stopped and did it for us. We arrived at the show in the nick of time, to find numerous beautiful greyhounds parading around. We'd had no idea there would be so many as we'd never showed a dog before. Imagine our surprise and delight when Poppy won her class of under two-year-old bitches, and then went on to win best bitch in show.

The judge said she was something special, and I should get her kennel club registered in order to show her properly at kennel club shows. We did, and she had considerable success. The highlight of her show career was winning Best Racing Bitch at Crufts in 2005 when she was eight-years old.

Sadly, we lost Poppy Jones in 2007, suddenly whilst out on a walk, but we now have Holly Hunter, another blue brindle bitch, who we've continued to show, and Holly has also had many successes in the show ring. She was placed at Crufts a couple of times, and most recently she won best over ten-year-old greyhound at the first Scottish greyhound gathering in July 2015. We are now completely besotted with this lovely breed and will never have any other.

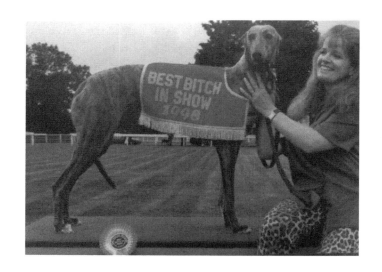

Bambi's Story - Carole Smith

In September 2000, whilst Stephen Redgrave, Tim Foster, Mathew Pinsent and James Cracknell were earning Olympic medals in the Sydney Olympic Games, a two-year-old Irish racing greyhound - a beautifully marked female brindle with snowflakes - travelled to the West of England from Ireland with her trainer to race at a West of England race meeting.

In Gloucestershire another trainer, Bob, who looked after greyhounds for other people, was taking hounds to the same race meeting. He and his wife had two young sons, and together they had great fun with the hounds in their care. Daily walks were a sight to behold, and the two little boys loved to run with the hounds, throwing an array of squeaky toys etc for them to catch.

However, the family's own beloved couch potato pet greyhound had just died and they were broken hearted.

In her race the Irish girl came second, and she was put up for auction. The bidding was keen and Bob, thinking this beautiful dog would be ideal as a replacement pet, joined in but was soon outbid. He was about to leave when another trainer came up to him and said, 'I saw you bidding for the Irish grey that I bought, do you want her? She's pulled a muscle in her leg and it will take months to bring her back to fitness, you can have her for nothing.' Bob took her home but soon realised that his family were not quite ready to have another pet, so she was put in the kennels to play with the other hounds and be entertained by the two little boys, who called her Bambi because she looked just like the Disney character.

My husband Gordon was an HGV tanker driver, a job he'd always wanted to do from when he was a small boy. He loved it; in fact he was a 'workaholic.'

At about the same time as the race meeting was taking place, Gordon, who was driving his car home from work, started having a seizure and pulled over onto the hard shoulder. He was admitted urgently to hospital where it was discovered that he had a brain tumour and the resulting effect meant that was the end of his career.

Greyhound trainer Bob is Gordon's nephew. Bob knew instantly that Gordon needed Bambi, and that Bambi needed him. Several times he asked, 'When are you coming to collect her?'

I eventually drove Gordon over just to see the dog, and we

agreed to take her. Bob gave us a list of instructions too. How to get her in/out of the car, how to persuade her to go into the house as she'd never set foot over a doorway, beware of cats as she'll most likely attack them...etc.

I opened the car door, sort of picked her up and unceremoniously hauled her in. She didn't growl, so task one was successful. On arriving home, we opened the car door and out she spilled - phew things were going well!

We unlocked the door, wondering if I'd have to push her inside or bribe her with something tasty, but she just strolled into the house like she'd been there for years, and plonked herself down in a corner of the room.

We fed her some food Bob had given us, opened the back door and she strolled into the garden to be met by our neighbours two cats! She looked at them, gave a deep sigh and completely ignored them. She did what she needed to do and went back inside to her corner.

The next morning, we came downstairs to find her sprawled, legs akimbo, on the sofa. She'd found her home!

At first it was my responsibility to walk her, but as his strength built up it became Gordon's duty, and soon there was a Bambi fan club in our local park, all carrying treats for when they saw her.

Then things changed. Bambi had been the only grey in the area, but a number of greys, whippets and lurchers appeared, giving her plenty of houndie friends to run with, although her best pal was our son's West Highland terrier!

Bambi lived until she was nine-years old. She was a kind, gentle dog who always gave extra time to those who were handicapped, and adjusted naturally to our grandchildren's arrival. When she passed over the Rainbow Bridge even the local cats came looking to see where their friend had gone. She helped us meet so many lovely people on our walks and even now they still often mention her. Rest easy our darling girl.

Jasmine's Story - Douglas Price

The plight of greyhounds isn't just happening in the UK. These beautiful dogs are suffering in many other countries too, such as Spain, Australia, and the USA.

This next story is from one of our American friends.

*

Our first experience with greyhounds came about as a result of pet sitting my son's greyhound, Annie. Annie was an extremely shy dog, who came out of her shell during the time she was with us. We absolutely fell in love with her and would have kept her if we could have.

Since keeping Annie was not an option, I headed off to the same greyhound adoption agency that Annie had come from - Project Racing Home in North Carolina, USA - to find another 'Annie'.

I found out that there wasn't another Annie there, but there were fifty other hounds all with their own unique personalities, likes, and dislikes! The adoption agency was very patient with me as I spent almost the whole day having a wonderful time meeting the hounds. Near the end of the day, after I had narrowed my list down to two or three hounds that seemed to be good fit for our home, I spotted a quiet female sitting in a kennel patiently looking at me with her beautiful, loving eyes. I asked about her and the adoption people said she didn't test well for someone as a first greyhound. She was an alpha female, very bossy and dominant.

I asked to see her anyway. I took her out to the yard and immediately we both knew that she was the one. We just communicated well together. She had been pointing towards the woods trying to tell someone about the foxes she had seen recently over there and nobody seemed to listen. I didn't know what she was pointing at until I later took her for a walk and found some footprints, but I knew enough to get down on one knee and listen to what she wanted to tell me.

I tried to look at one more hound after I saw her - notice I said 'tried.' She was having none of that, she howled and barked like mad in her kennel. This greyhound had chosen me to be her adoptee and that was the way it was going to be. Her racing name was SK Snowflake, but we changed it to Jasmine as it seemed to suit her better.

Sometimes, bringing a greyhound who has known nothing but kennel life into a home situation can be difficult. They are used to being in the company of other dogs and living a very structured life - five a.m. wake ups every morning, etc. Jasmine's transition was fairly easy because we were pet sitting Annie and Jax - a lurcher - for the next two weeks, and had resident Lucky - an old spaniel - so we had a ready-made pack for Jasmine to boss around when she got home.

Jasmine has been a joyous addition to our family. She goes everywhere with us. This particular greyhound likes hiking, which is good because it encourages the wife and me to get out and exercise more often. It seems that all greyhounds have their own little weird idiosyncrasies. One of Jasmine's, that we find both amusing and puzzling, is that she loves to walk in the little shopping centres where grocery stores are located - we call them strip malls in the states. Jasmine loves to meet people. It doesn't matter whether we're on a hike, at a bar, out shopping, out doing anything, she wants to meet you!

We've had days when people seemed either unfriendly, or scared of her size, and no one came over to visit. She would sulk because her feelings were hurt because no one came over to talk to her. Jasmine loves to chase balls and play fetch, however, she is very afraid of snakes, spiders, and lizards of any size.

In summary, I'd have to say that this greyhound has enriched our lives tremendously, and we are very glad that she chose us to go home with.

Judd's Story - Ann Raynor

We've always had lurchers, but I've always wanted a greyhound for some reason. I think they are such beautiful creatures, just perfect, so, when my terrier died, leaving my small lurcher all alone, I told my hubby we were going to get a grey. Luckily he feels the same as me and loves them, so we rang up the Retired Greyhound Trust in our local area.

We arranged a date for a home check, which we passed, then went to along to look for a new fur baby.

It wasn't that easy though! Every hound we looked at acted like it wanted to eat my small long-haired lurcher, not one of them seemed to accept her.

I was really upset, but then Sandra – the lady who runs the kennels - said, 'I think I have the perfect boy for you,' and out came Mick. A beautiful black hound with white legs and a white face, I loved his markings, they were just like those on my horse. And, most importantly, he got on well with our lurcher.

Sandra told us Mick had previously had an accident – a group of hounds were doing zoomies and somehow they all piled into each other - and he'd dislocated his spine, but was on the mend. He'd been wearing a muzzle during the accident, which had pushed the skin off his face and he was quite badly scarred by it.

But that didn't put us off; we fell in love with him and agreed to take him home.

Initially, he would scream if you put your face near his, maybe it was traumatic memories of the accident, but with time and patience he got over his fear.

We've had him for five years now, and he is truly the best dog. He seems to have forgotten his past, and is such an affectionate boy. He's obsessed with cuddles and kisses; in fact he actually claws you for a hug and attention.

He is my whole world. He's so well behaved and rarely puts a foot wrong.

We renamed him Judd, after my love of Poldark.

He's ten-years old now. I hope and pray we have him for another five years.

I count myself really lucky to have found him that day.

Gemma, Pamela, Ronnie and Frosty's Story – Suzy Decodts

We adopted Gemma first, not a name we would have chosen, but at two-years old it seemed wrong to change it. As the years passed we gifted her with many permutations of her name. Gemily, and Princess Gemmalina, were the most used, along, of course with DLG - Daddy's Little Girl.

The adoption, as it is in so many cases, was all my idea. Our son was now high school age and rapidly growing up and away. Mid forties, and home all day due to a combination of reasons, I yearned to share my days with another little one and my wish was granted more fully than I ever anticipated.

Gemma came to us on 8 August 2011. A dark, dainty little sprite, she moved with all the grace of a ballerina. At first she was shy and afraid to show any attachment, but she soon blossomed and began to show us love in return.

I worried that she might be lonely so put plans in place to find her a sister. It took over a year before Pamela was placed with us, and then within a few short months we were told that Pamela's brother, Ronnie was also looking for a home. How could we say no?

It turned out that Ronnie was the catalyst. Both girls were fairly quiet and reserved, so we were quite unprepared for the exuberance and unrestrained energy that Ronnie brought.

At first I was horrified, but it was the turning point for Pamela, who up until then had been a bit of a withdrawn scaredy cat. Almost immediately she was transformed from a nervy dog to a calm, confident one.

I write about my hounds as though they are children, but for us they have become so. They have brought us very nearly as much happiness as children bring to a family. Their joy when we return home is boundless, the waggy tails, play bows and yowly growliness lifts my spirits like nothing else.

To us they are the perfect pet. They are gentle and calm for most of the day. They don't pull on the lead when walking, and are generally well behaved. If I was seventy instead of fifty, I think I could still manage one.

They are incredibly funny in the little things they do.

I buy their food in fifteen-kilo sacks, and Ronnie will tuck the bag up so that visiting hounds don't steal his food. We only have to tell him that Billy is coming, and he trots off to check the bag is closed. What bad manners!

They are not a breed of dog that barks a lot. I've had Gemma for five years, and not heard her bark once.

Ronnie and Pamela will bark, yowl and growl in a seeming attempt to communicate with us but never when we are out. In fact it was years before our neighbours even noticed we had them.

Frosty Lee was the last dog we adopted. He was a beautiful black hound speckled with white snowflakes. He had the waggiest tail of all our hounds but took the longest time to settle in. It wasn't that he didn't want to, he just didn't know how. Poor little Frosty had spent seven years living the kennel life. He didn't understand home living at all; he found it overwhelming at first. He would try and snatch food from the fridge whenever I opened the door, he stole my father's sandwich as soon as it was made, and would leap up on the table or the worktops to get the first treat. The naughtiest thing he did was steal a whole boiled ham. I saw him looking at it and told him NO! He looked at me, then back at the ham, no more than six inches away from his nose and made his choice.

Now he's gone, I'm glad he had the ham.

Before he died, Frosty calmed down and became one of us. He fitted in beautifully. He was so easy to please, it was heart-warming. He loved tennis balls with a passion that bordered on obsession. He saw a pack of three squeaky Kong tennis balls at the vet's once, and barked at them longingly until I bought them. Unfortunately, once we reached home he'd killed them all within minutes, leaving chewed up rubber pieces.

I then ordered a box of fifty used tennis balls from eBay and unwrapped them in front of him. It was pandemonium at first, he was so excited and so was I. Whichever direction I threw the balls, he would leap in the air and catch them. It was amazing.

Sadly the balls outlived him and the last one remains, along with his collar on the box where his ashes lie.

I promised to take him to the seaside and I will keep my promise the next time I visit Devon.

He was the waggiest of all my hounds and I miss him dreadfully.

It's only three months since he died, quickly and without

much pain on his part. I was with him as he died, holding his little paw and telling him I loved him. We kept him at home for another day, snuggled on the sofa where he'd died, giving us time to accept our loss. All the hounds said goodbye and I sat beside him the whole night, stroking his cooling fur. I've never felt like this over a dog before but there is something special about these hounds. No matter how much it hurt losing Frosty, we will continue to rescue/rehome these hounds. It is our tribute to him.

I am horrified that thousands of these gentle loving creatures are put to death each year simply because they don't come first in the races. It makes me feel sick - so sick I can't think about it, or I would go to pieces. In my heart I know that the four we've adopted have freed up four places for hounds that could have been euthanised. I wish I could do more and that is why I've written our story.

I hope that more people will realise just how lovely these hounds are, and find some space in their lives to give one a home.

I know that when we go to bed tonight, my husband will lean across to give me a goodnight kiss and Ronnie will lift up his head to join in the kiss, as he does every night. We love them and they adore us, and for that moment, all is right with the world.

Bonnie and Indie's Story - Katharine Jane Hardisty

We all know that once you've met a greyhound, you will never quite get over it. Once you understand the worldwide plight of greyhounds, you will never be able to ignore it and choose a 'normal' dog. They say, when a greyhound steals your heart, it's like you become a member of a cult! It seems to be more of an addiction than the simply reality of having a pet dog.

My beautiful Bonnie was chosen for me by the wonderful local rehoming officer at GRWE (Greyhound Rescue West of England). I am certain a more perfect match wouldn't be possible.

Having lived with Bonnie for over a year - and fallen totally head over heels - I began to worry about what life would be like for me when the inevitable happens and she has to leave me. Obviously, I hope that day will be a very long time away, but you never know what's around the corner. My self-preservation plan - and my new found addiction to greyhounds - was to think about adopting another one.

Beautiful Bonnie had already opened up a whole new wonderful world for me. I've met so many lovely new friends - both in real life and on-line - and I'm more than willing to do whatever volunteer work I can to help other hounds find their forever sofas.

During this time I discovered Galgos del Sol, an amazing rescue based in Murcia, Spain, that is passionately dedicated to the rescue and rehabilitation of abandoned and injured galgos - also known as Spanish greyhounds.

http://www.galgosdelsol.org/

At the end of March 2014, it was reported that a heavily pregnant galga was just about surviving alone in the streets. She wouldn't initially allow herself be caught.

It wasn't long before she'd given birth and still wouldn't be caught. One of the rescuers wasn't sure whether to take the pups or not as it was a high-risk area. It was possible these pure breed galgo pups would be taken by the wrong people. It was a very difficult situation and very frustrating. The mother was feeding the pups in the street and too many people knew that she - and they - were there.

Locals said she'd been on the streets for a long time and had given birth this way before. None of these previous litters of pups were known to have survived.

About a day later, and thanks to GdS volunteers, they were all finally safe and on their way to care, comfort, food, water and love, at the rescue centre. They called the mother, Pumpkin, and her little ones were known as pumpkin seeds.

Poor Pumpkin's ears and body were covered in fleas and ticks. She was so skinny and must have felt terrible. Sadly, only six of the original eight babies survived.

The only safe, secure place available to put the dog and her pups was Tina's bathroom. Tina is the founder, and President, of GdS.

Once Pumpkin was settled, she appeared to improve a little and her beautiful little babes began to thrive. Sadly, even with all the food, care and attention, Pumpkin just wasn't well enough to continue with six hungry mouths to feed, so Tina and the lovely volunteers had to take over with eight feeds a day!

With the additional rest, Pumpkin appeared to have a nice life for a while. Lots of relaxing, some medication, and plenty of good food. Sadly, no one could have guessed her health was deteriorating so badly. She was beginning to look healthier and was ready to be spayed with a view to finding her forever sofa.

Pumpkin was at the vets, sedated and ready for her operation, when the vet realised she was completely riddled with cancer, and sadly poor Tina had to go to say good-bye to an already anaesthetised Pumpkin. We all kissed her good-night, we all wished her the very sweetest of dreams over the Rainbow Bridge, and we all promised to keep her beautiful pumpkin seeds safe, happy, healthy, and totally spoiled for the rest of their days.

The puppies were gorgeous and every day I checked the GdS Facebook page for updates to see how they were doing. One by one, these beautiful babies were being reserved. All except one little black girlie called Indie.

I just had to send Tina a message to ask if there was anyone interested in little Indie pumpkin seed. Tina's answer was yes, me! So that was that.

Following The Big Decision, I had six weeks of doubt, anguish, planning, panicking and preparing to do. The biggest worry was wondering just how Bonnie was going to react. After all, I had no idea what Indie's personality was like.

Would Bonnie accept this little intruder? Knowing just how loving Bonnie is, I had high hopes.

During the time I was waiting for Indie's travel date to arrive, I kept a close eye on all the photos and FB posts about the pups. In nearly every picture of them, Indie was in the background, just watching; whilst all her rowdy siblings were jumping up at the fences and leaping all over the GdS volunteers. She seemed to be an observer, not at all a dominant character, and this endeared her to me even more. I think I was totally in love with her way before we ever met!

The time between my decision to offer Indie a home, and Monday 21 July 2014 was the longest six weeks of my life. To help pass the time, I set up a FB page called 'The Pumpkin Seeds' for all the new mums and dads to post pictures and stories of the development of this lovely litter of rescued pups. I thought there may be a few GdS supporters keen to see the babies in their new homes, but I am so very proud that our little page has over 650 followers to date, and it's still growing.

The day I was due to meet Indie, I received communication from the transport that our rendezvous would be quite late at night and about 130 miles away.

Eventually, I met my darling, teeny, four-month-old Indie at nearly midnight, on a junction roundabout off the M4.

It was like a dodgy drug deal!

I showed my ID and the van driver opened a cage in the back of his van enabling me to scoop up my tiny little girl. She was less than nine kilos with no muscle tone. She seemed so very timid, tiny and fragile.

This was the beginning of a fantastic relationship. Not just between Indie and me, but after a couple of weeks, darling Bonnie began to respond to Indie's playful advances, and soon they were the very best of friends.

My lovely girlies show me complete unconditional love. They make my smile every day. They've stamped their paw prints firmly on my heart, and will always be my number one priority. I also try to do whatever I can to help to raise funds for both the charities who found my lovely dogs for me. I wish I could do more, and I wish I could rehome more lovely greyhounds.

Pepper's Story – Stephanie Patterson

My mother and I arrived in the UK with half a plane-load of pets - four cats and two dogs, to be precise.

After the initial excitement of starting life in a new country - well, apart from seeing our 'babies' cooped up in quarantine, a horrible experience for them and us - the sad times began.

First we lost Kater, our fifteen-year-old tomcat, to cancer during the last few days in confinement. In May 1997, Polly, a former feral cat, disappeared a couple of days after we moved into our idyllic countryside home in Kent, leaving not a trace. And a few months later, Sheila, my six-year-old rescue cat, was hit by a car and passed away. We were gutted.

Harmony reigned for about a year, with our two large mongrels, Pascha and Bear, and my one remaining cat, Gizmo. But sadly, in June 1998, Pascha, our shepherd-wolf mix, succumbed to the after-effects of kennel cough. He was an older lad who didn't want to leave us, but he couldn't fight it off forever. We buried him in a newly created rockery in our garden. Bear was inconsolable. Pascha had been like a father to him when he arrived at our home as a puppy a few years earlier. The two had been inseparable. For weeks, Bear walked around the spot in our living room where Pascha had died, looking gloomy.

So, two months on, my mother decided it was time to look for a friend for Bear. She visited the Last Chance Animal Rescue Centre, in Edenbridge, Kent, and a few days later Pepper, a black greyhound with a sprinkling of grey all over, came to join us. The charity still picks up former racing greyhounds from the infamous pounds in Wales, where the dogs are kept in appalling conditions.

On his arrival, Pepper was in a pitiful state: skin and bones, with sores and lesions all over his legs and ribcage, and his paws raw. We cried at the injustice and the barbaric trade in dogs for racing. Sadly, to this day, racing dog owners still dump the dogs when they don't perform anymore. Why aren't they pursued?

We still have photos from Pepper's first day in our garden, tentatively exploring his new realm. Bear wasn't too happy at first, but he must have sensed Pepper's insecurities, and gave him space.

After a few days, Pepper began to settle in, and to show his cheeky nature! I kept some fluffy toys on my sofa - some that Pascha had loved to play with, much to my annoyance - and Pepper showed a keen interest in them. One morning, he grabbed Pascha's favourite fluffy toy - how on earth did he know? - went into the garden, and placed it on top of the rockery below which Pascha was buried. Bear was with him. They lay down beside it, chuffed with their achievement. To say we were amazed is an understatement. To us, it felt like Pascha approved. It was a laugh and cry moment.

Over the months, Pepper turned into a handsome, well-fed and happy dog. He loved to run across the fields behind the house - for about ten minutes. Then, he was keen to return home for a snooze on his sofa. It's funny how you can cope with sitting on the edge of a sofa with a happily snoring dog sprawled on his back taking up most of the space. Pepper and Bear were mirror images. We didn't mind, really...

No scrap of food was safe from Pepper - he had been starved, after all, that was his excuse! - So everything from biscuits to fruit had to be kept out of reach. He would try to open cupboard doors and poke his long nose into the tiniest gaps. He pinched your breakfast toast from your hand when you didn't pay attention, and you had to tell him to lie down in order to enjoy your (his?) dinner. He was such a character! You just couldn't bear a grudge.

After I moved to Scotland with Gizmo, I only ever saw Pepper when I visited several times a year. One such occasion was around Christmas time. With me I brought not only Gizmo, but also Mouse, a fluffy six-month-old kitten. And whilst Pepper was used to Gizmo, this tiny grey meowing bundle intrigued him, especially when it bounced down the stairs. So, to keep a close eye on his new friend, Pepper in his perpetual curiosity poked his nose through the banister rails, sniffing excitedly, only to receive a swipe of tiny, sharp claws across his nose. Oh, the indignity! Mouse stared at him, completely unfazed, whilst Pepper howled and barked at him, unable to get over the insult. You would think that by then Pepper knew to keep his nose out of trouble. Not quite so...

One anecdote of his adventures I'm told by my mother is that a few years later, in the middle of the night to Boxing Day - I wasn't visiting that time - she woke up to a crunching sound. Worried that someone might be in the house, she woke her partner, and together they bravely ventured into the corridor. They couldn't believe their eyes: Pepper was lying on the floor, happily crunching the bones of a turkey carcass. Now, my mother hadn't cooked turkey that Christmas…

It turned out that Pepper had somehow managed to sneak out of her enclosed garden - no idea how - gone into the neighbour's garden - no idea how - and pulled the turkey carcass from their wheelie bin before proudly carrying his trophy home! Needless to say, Pepper had a fine nose for scents…and a healthy appetite for turkey leftovers.

During his life with my mother, Pepper later moved to Italy for a couple of years - where my husband saved him from falling into a river in his excitement, but that's another story - and from there to Germany, where my mother cared for my elderly grandmother, who hadn't had a dog in her home since my mother was a toddler. Pepper always enjoyed his walkies by the river, even when mostly blind, and he never lost his cheeky, mischievous nature.

Sadly, Pepper had to be put to sleep at the wonderful age of sixteen, almost completely blind and with serious arthritis. Apart from hell during the first few years as a racing greyhound, he enjoyed a fantastic life of leisure with us. He always kept us on our toes, was the sweetest dog you can imagine - apart from when he 'released' air when stretched on his back on the sofa - and he had a wicked sense for adventure that got him into trouble on a number of occasions. We will always miss him.

PS: My mother adopted a German shepherd called Morpheus a couple of months after Pepper's departure, continuing the family tradition of giving a rescue pet a good home.

Patsy's Story – Lorna Gray

Somehow, lovely as they are, Labradors, collies or spaniels were never more than a one-second possibility. Having already got a lurcher, Hamish, as our first dog, and still getting used to his daft post-puppy ways, we were definite that to complete our 'family' we needed a calm dog. We kept thinking how lovely greyhounds were. So, we started to look on the Greyhound Rescue West of England website and we saw two year old Patsy. It said she was 'Princess Patsy, born to live in a home.' She was a black beauty; alert and sleek and obviously built for speed. Funny how no-one had ever told her that! A lazier dog you would find it hard to meet! So, this is the story of our first meeting and our first months with Patsy.

A fresh autumn day dawned, and with Hamish in the car, we set off from West Sussex for Kent where Patsy was being fostered by a lady called Kaye. We never assumed we wouldn't be bringing her home, so everything was ready…pink collar, harness and lead and pink tag for our own doggy daughter!

We introduced Hamish to Patsy in Kaye's huge garden, and all went well. Indoors, my husband Bill promptly fell in love with the prettiest pair of brown eyes. He sat down on the floor by Patsy - as all loyal subjects should for a princess - and that was it! Meantime, Hamish marked the stair area, just to remind us that he was still number one dog. Oh, the embarrassment!

After coffee and a chat with Kaye, we signed the papers and Janet from GRWE said Patsy was ours. To get home, Hamish went in his boot crate, and Patsy was supposed to lay on the back seat with me; although she didn't quite manage it By the time we got home, she had slipped between the front seat and the back seat and was lying good humouredly in the ungainliest of poses; long legs sticking up as she tried and failed to right herself. After endless wriggles - and crossed fingers from us that she wouldn't break a leg before we even returned home - all was well.

That first week with Patsy, we realised how different she was to Hamish, whose way of dealing with worries was to bark. Not long out of kennels, many household activities worried her, including the television. Any squeaks or meows on adverts sent her flying to the set, where she attempted to find the culprit disturbing her peace. Every evening she lay with ears up, ready to pounce. Further 'problems' followed. Leaves skimming the patio roof were enough to send Patsy into a state of high anxiety, and not far behind them on the fear-scale was rain on the windows, high winds, and...cobwebs. I never knew we had so many in our Victorian house until she pointed them all out to me! More extreme was Patsy's fear of thunder and fireworks. We stopped buying ourselves treats and bought thundershirts, pheromone sprays, and de-sensitising CDs.

On road walks, Hamish gave Patsy some confidence, but she would suddenly freeze, dig in her paws and wait for inspiration. Finally, after many painfully slow walks, we chanced on using a squeaker to propel her along the pavement. But would she poop? No! It took many weeks of encouragement and excited suggestions of, 'Go wee, Patsy. Go poo.'

If the neighbours had any doubts about our sanity, they were now confirmed. The first time she pooped on a woodland walk, we celebrated.

We've now had Patsy for nearly four years, and we love her more each day. She rarely runs, but loves her walks; cuddles; tummy tickles; food, window-watching and digging holes. She bounds in and out of rooms excitedly when the lead comes out and storms ahead of Hamish now! There is little left of that nervous girl. But, cobwebs? Well, I still have to keep the dusters busy!

Lightning's Story – Bernadette Cole

In March 2011 we fostered the shyest greyhound I had ever met.

Lightning - racing name Black Topper - was initially very shy and quite aloof when people tried to say hello. He came to temporarily live with Toots, Clover, and Bailey, making him the fourth dog in our household.

In June that year, we decided our house was going to become Lightning's forever home, or I should say, Lightning chose us.

As time went on he became better with people and with other dogs too.

In October of the same year, we decided to foster again, and as Lightning was so good with other breeds of dog we decided to try German Shepherds.

Quattro came to live with us; and for the first two or three months everything went smoothly, until Quattro barged into Lightning one day and a fight happened. Needless to say Lightning came out hurt and traumatised from this encounter, so Quattro had to go.

We stopped fostering for a while and then we heard about a beautiful black greyhound in need of a foster home. We jumped at the chance, as we thought another greyhound would be great for Lightning.

Jet arrived, and for the first six weeks there were no problems between him and Lightning. Then my husband Richard's parents – Yvonne and Peter - came to stay and we put all the dogs into the hall to give them time to settle. Next thing, there was a lot of barking and growling from the hall. Jet and Lightning were fighting.

Poor Lightning was very badly hurt. He had an open wound in his chest and torn muscle as well. Jet on the other hand was fine with just a couple of cuts.

Peter and I spent the next five hours at the vets. Because I'm a trained veterinary assistant, I was allowed to help the vet operate on Lightning, and for two hours I had my hands in his chest, fighting for his life. At that stage I would have sold my soul for that hound to recover. After the surgery, we were worried sick as it took him another two hours to come around from the anaesthetic.

We nursed Lightening for the next three months. His chest had to heal as an open wound because there wasn't enough skin to pull together over the injury.

Lightning is well now, but he still finds it hard to trust other dogs, especially if they are in his space, and will give a warning growl if they get too close.

I can imagine you all thinking, what happened to Jet? I can tell you that Jet went to another foster home, and then to his forever home as an only dog.

We are now three years on from that dreadful experience, and Lightning is a very happy greyhound who sleeps for at least eighteen hours a day. His favourite place to sleep during the day is on the couch, and at night, on our bed.

If you ever want to meet Lightning, he can be found at various walks in Devon, with his pals Toots, Clover, Bailey, and our new addition, Guinness, another greyhound.

Frank's Story – Jane McCarthy

Several years ago my husband decided he wanted us to get a family pet. He really wanted a dog, a greyhound in particular as he'd heard that they made great pets, and he wanted to give a rescue greyhound a home.

We'd heard lots of horror stories about how they are treated whilst racing and then just dumped after they stop making money for the owners and trainers.

I was a bit apprehensive initially as we both worked and knew we couldn't be there all the time for a new dog, but my husband kept on, and he also got our two children on his side.

I still resisted, but after being in our local town centre one day, and seeing a lady with two greyhounds which my husband adored, I agreed to go to our local dogs trust to have a look only.

That was in December 2011, and by January 2012 I relented, and we picked up Frank, our then three-year-old brindle boy.

With the help of the children, who were at college and school, we worked out a dog sitting rota until we found we could leave him for longer.

He's our gentle giant at 38 kg and 29 inches in height to his shoulder, but we wouldn't be without him. We've had so much fun, learning what all the strange noises he makes mean, and realising that greyhounds don't need loads of exercise and are really couch potatoes.

He's had a few scrapes, such as running into the patio door whilst it was closed, but thankfully he didn't do any damage to himself or the door, not that you'd know it by the noise he made. Greyhounds do this thing called a GSOD, which stands for Greyhound Scream of Death, and they really do scream. It's such a frightening noise because you think they must be dying, but it's often for the silliest of things, like a piece of paper blowing at them! On another occasion, he got his tail trapped in a door and had to have it partially amputated, and he's also started to suffer with a corn, which we are soaking and moisturising. He is - in the vet's words – 'A big fairy.' He won't go into the consulting room at the vets without making a fuss, and that's before they even look at him!

We now think about everything we do. When we go on holiday, we find a dog friendly cottage and take Frank with us, and we've bought a car with a bigger boot area for him.

Frank was very nervous when we first got him, so we think he may have been mistreated, but he's learnt to trust us now and he allows us to do more with him, although he's still nervous at times.

We've had him for three and half years now, and our lives have changed, or I should say, we have adjusted our lives so we can give Frank a good, happy home. He has lots of love, plenty of food and treats and a comfy bed - or two or three, depending on whose bedroom he can get into first - and we love him so much even when he's naughty. All he has to do is look longingly at us with his puppy dog eyes, and our hearts melt.

Stan's Story – Sarah Tyrrell Jones

Blue our rescued greyhound/Alsatian cross was thriving. He was now two-years old and had settled in well. I'd also found a lovely boyfriend, and my nine-year-old son was growing up.

My boyfriend mentioned that maybe Blue needed a companion since I was working more.

I thought why not? Blue was easy going and maybe he did need the company of another dog.

So, at the weekend, we went to the local rescue centre. As soon as we got there I knew it wasn't going to be pleasant. The owner was shouting at the staff, I couldn't see where the dogs were exercised, and it smelled bad.

We had to pay to get in, which I didn't mind as hopefully the money went to helping the dogs, but it was the way we were spoken to that wasn't nice...sharp and rudely.

The owner shouted at us, 'Bet you've come for a nose round like all others.'

'No,' I replied, 'we were wondering if you had any greyhounds or cross breeds as...'

I was cut off mid sentence.

'In there,' the owner pointed, and she stormed off.

We walked into a large farm like building. Every dog was quiet...this didn't feel right.

The dogs were sat in their baskets looking at us from their enclosure. I cried because they all looked so sad, and said, 'Craig I have to go.'

We rushed out and gulped the fresh air. At that moment, a very skinny half greyhound half whippet limped around the corner. He was lucky as he was only just being brought in.

Craig and I looked at each other, and without saying a word I walked up to the person holding him and told them I was taking him home. I picked the dog up, and Craig literally ran to the car.

'Get in,' he said.

The owner looked at me, and all she said was, 'Yeah take him.'

We drove home and put the dog in the kitchen. Blue knew straight away that this dog needed some TLC.

My son, Joe, said, 'Mum why have you bought me a see-

107

through dog?'

The poor thing was so skinny you could see his veins in his legs. He'd also been burned.

Joe said, 'Let's call him Ronaldo.'

'I shook my head. Joe then said, 'Mum, can we call him Stanly?'

Stan's now ten, and he and Blue are soul mates.

Stan's injuries healed really well and he put on weight. Bless him, he's still got a limp, a wonky nose and is blind in one eye, but to us he's just perfect.

Hamish's Story – Lorna Gray

My husband Bill and I thought about getting a greyhound; a quiet, gentle dog that didn't need huge amounts of exercise. We vigorously researched greyhounds and their needs, and as we started looking at websites, we found Greyhound Rescue West of England. I sent long emails of bullet-point questions to Janet, the re-homing officer, and she kindly replied with equally long answers.

A greyhound would definitely suit our life-style. We passed the home-check, and were ready to re-home one, except we didn't!

A small, brindle lurcher, around fourteen-months old kept looking out from the lap-top, in a series of fun-filled photos. He was running, or rolling in the grass - and maybe more - or catching toys, but he was rarely still for long. We were not daunted, not us. After all, if I could teach thirty infants, surely a young lurcher would be simple enough? We travelled to the kennels.

'Don't be put off, they can be a bit excited coming out,' we were warned. They were right!

Our first sight of Hamish was of an open-mouthed, energetic bundle; tongue lolling, and legs pulling sideways crab-fashion. We just stared. During the walk, we decided we were actually rather taken with Sox, the small, quiet whippet.

We decided to think about it.

That week, every day, we stared at Hamish on the website. GRWE assured us he would settle down with a firm hand and clear boundaries.

We weakened, and a week later, on a lovely autumn day, we were reunited with Hamish on a Sighthounds Group walk. We drove home, with Diana Krall crooning away on the CD player, and introduced our skinny, brindle, new best friend to our Victorian, city house. He quickly asked to go out – a good sign - and settled down for a post-dinner nap. That night, we did as suggested and took him to his bed, closed the door, and retired. He cried. We hid our heads under pillows. He whined more. After an hour, we realised he wasn't going to stop and we decided to go against the advice and get him.

Suddenly, something came charging up the stairs. Hamish had undone the tight brass handle on the door of his 'isolation cell,' and was bounding towards us! He leapt on the bed, snapping the air, in true Hannibal Lecter style.

'I'd better take him out for a wee,' I said.

He happily did that and then calmly trotted along to his new bed...on the landing!

That was the start of our very eventful life with a cheeky lurcher. In the first few weeks, we realised that he had a penchant for slippers and wasn't at all keen to part with them when asked to. No toy was safe; they were all ragged, gutted and well and truly 'dead.' He ate his harness rather than let us put it on him. He had no 'off switch', and as we got more used to him, and he us, we realised he couldn't cope on-lead with dogs, motor-bikes, buses, white vans and Land Rovers. Not quite the dog we were expecting!

However, Hamish excelled at games, moving from side to side, footballer fashion, paw raised, waiting for Bill to throw the ball again and again. He eventually learned phrases like 'drop it', but stuffed his paws in his floppy ears at 'leave it' or 'move,' and my seat on the sofa was coveted and gripped on to with a low growl for the first six months at least.

Luckily, reward-based training tapped into Hamish's natural greed and helped us overcome most obstacles. Eventually, we realised that we needed professional help with his reactivity, and he made slow, but steady progress with counter-conditioning. Despite his problems, his occasional naughtiness and extreme cheekiness, Hamish is the most loving hound, with beautiful warm brown eyes, and he follows us everywhere with his tail wagging.

He's taught himself to fetch a toy to chew on if he feels over-excited, and to go on his bed and wait when a visitor comes. He sleeps all evening and all through the night, sprints like a rocket, and can play happily off-lead in an enclosed area with all different breeds of dog. He knows a huge number of words, and even the spellings we replaced them with, so we can no longer say 's-t-r-o-l-l' for 'walk.' He smiles at us when we return home on the rare occasions we go anywhere, and now, aged five, he is still a puppy at heart. We love him to bits and we wouldn't want him any other way.

Paddy's Story – Charlotte Stockley

I got a phone call late one night in November 2006, asking if I would foster an eight-week-old greyhound puppy from a racing kennels over the Christmas period. All his siblings had homes, but he was too little to stay in kennels on his own. I talked it over with my husband and we decided that yes, we would foster him until a home came along, and we were sure it wouldn't be long.

We went to the kennels to collect him at the beginning of December, and armed with a borrowed crate and instructions on how often to feed him, we travelled home with him wrapped up in a blanket in a box on my knee.

At home it was like Little and Large when we introduced Paddy – the name given to the pup - to Drum and Neva, our other greyhounds, as he was so small.

We set the crate up and let Paddy out into the garden to explore. The first thing he did was run after Drum who went around the pond, and Paddy landed in it with a big splash! Trying not to laugh we pulled him out and dried him off before letting him try again. This time he missed the pond.

Over the next few days, things settled down, and everyone got used to having a mini hurricane around. Paddy's crate became his own little space with his toys and bed and anything else he decided needed to be there. He was brilliant with his toileting and always clean in the house.

Just before Christmas I had a phone call to say some people were interested in adopting him and were attending an arranged greyhound walk between Christmas and New Year to meet him. We took him to meet family over the festive season and everyone loved him to bits.

His prospective owners had passed their home check, and were planning on taking Paddy home in mid January. They loved him and said they definitely wanted him. A date was set and on the day I packed his things, wrote a letter detailing his routine and took him to meet his new family. I will admit to sobbing the whole way home after leaving him.

Three weeks later I got a phone call from the rescue centre. The family wanted to return Paddy as he was dirty in the house, so would we have him back as a foster again? We immediately said yes and arranged to pick him up. He was so pleased to see us, and didn't let us out of his sight for a few days after we got him back home.

I have no idea what the family had done to Paddy, but we could no longer use a crate as he howled constantly. The only way we could get him to sleep was to put a bed under our bed for him.

It became obvious fairly quickly that the three weeks he'd been with them had not been good for him. He hadn't put on any weight, and he was now fearful of things that previously hadn't bothered him. It didn't take much for us to decide to keep him.

We booked him in for puppy classes with the lovely trainer we'd taken Drum and Neva to, and went from there.

Over the years we've had a number of problems with his behaviour. He hates other dogs and cats, and if he's afraid of something he just goes into defence mode and growls and snarls until he is left alone.

Paddy is now nearly nine, and was diagnosed as being autistic in March 2014, which explained most of his odd behaviour. Since being diagnosed he's been treated by an expert vet in this field and has come on in leaps and bounds. He's now better able to cope with life.

He is so loving, and adores people. He's made an amazing Pets as Therapy dog too.

Right now he is curled up on his bed next to my desk with his head resting on my foot. While he hasn't been the easiest dog on the planet I wouldn't change him for the world.

Raffi's Story – Ann Ward

Although we liked dogs, we'd never really taken much notice of greyhounds. All I knew was that they were skinny dogs.

Initially we lived in a flat, but after we moved into our house, we had more space and I decided I'd like a dog, and I knew there was a local Retired Greyhound Trust kennels, so we went there one day out of curiosity, and ended up taking the dogs for a walk every Sunday.

It was lovely to see different hounds being adopted each week, except for one, called Raffi. Nobody seemed to want him; he was always left behind for some reason.

After several months, we asked if we could adopt him, and were taken with Raffi to a local park to see how he reacted to other dogs. It worried me a bit as he seemed quite aggressive towards other breeds. Maybe that was why he was always being overlooked?

But it didn't put us off him, we still took him home, and with time he became a different dog all together.

We had Raffi for six and a half years, and loved him to bits. He became the child we never had, and was a wonderful dog.

After a while, we thought maybe Raffi would like a canine companion, so we decided to foster, and were given Chloe, who happened to be Raffi's sister. Well, she was only with us for thirty-six hours before we knew we wanted to adopt her, and in June 2013, she became ours, making our family complete. She and Raffi got on so well, they were always playing together in the garden and in our bedroom with their teddies.

Unfortunately, Raffi died a few months ago, but we will always cherish the memories of our time with him, the happy moments and the sad.

We've kept Raffi's ashes, so we feel that he's still with us, and his memory lives on. We've still got Chloe, which helps ease the grief a bit. I'm so glad we visited the RGT out of curiosity that day; otherwise we'd never have known what wonderful pets greyhounds make.

Ranger's Story – Toby Johnson

I remember the walks - peaceful evenings with him by my side, his long easy stride that had no problem keeping pace with mine whether I chose to run, jog or stroll.

His name was Ranger, a big brindle boy who'd come into my life to replace a friend recently passed. Ranger was another greyhound, for no other dog could fill the place deep in my heart that was hurting.

At first, all I felt was that he wasn't my old friend, Baron, he was new and different, and maybe getting him had been a mistake, maybe it was too soon?

He came from the race tracks, just as his predecessor had, now too broken to compete; a dislocated shoulder had put paid to his racing days.

I remember how pleased his former owner had been at finding a forever home for him, and how glad I'd been to take him into mine.

He was a little underweight, but plenty of good food soon fixed that, and as the days passed he began to fill the hurt with his gentle friendship.

With exercise, discipline and affection, we built a new bond. I showed him that not everything that crossed his path was to be chased, and he relaxed into a more mellow mind-set rather than the edgy racing one he'd initially come to me with.

I think after a few weeks it dawned on him that he was retired from all that and while I'm sure he missed it - as the many times he tried to break into a full blooded sprint testified - they were soon curtailed by a yelp of pain as his bad shoulder strained under the unexpected pressure, and he stopped short. I would then massage his sore limb while chastising him for being a silly dog!

He soon settled into our new routine. After a time he stopped trying to be a racer, though he always had the better of me.

Many people say a greyhound needs little exercise and don't like long distance jogs, but this became Ranger's new passion. Together we started jogging along the quiet country roads. Pounding the tarmac come rain or shine, I started to feel fitter and healthier as Ranger pushed me harder. But as many dog lovers know, our four legged companions wear out faster than we do. As Ranger got older, his bad leg got stiffer, so he no longer wished to jog, preferring a short walk. Long nights in front of the fire were his new passion, and I was happy to indulge my old friend for I knew his time with me was coming to an end.

Many years have passed since Ranger left me, and while I've had several dogs since, I haven't had another greyhound. Whether this is because Baron and Ranger were such good friends to me I'm worried I won't find that again, I don't know, but maybe it is time to start jogging again and give one of these wondrous hounds a new forever home?

*** Editor's note – yes, Toby, definitely!

Taffy's Story – Jane Attenborough

A family trip to Battersea Dogs Home one May Bank Holiday in 2005, to look for a medium sized family dog to help get me out and about walking twice daily rather than sitting in front of the telly, resulted in us coming home with Adam, a rather large, quiet brindle greyhound boy who had - according to Battersea - come to them from a farm or kennels in Wales.

Adam jumped straight into the back of my 4x4 - forever known after that as the 'houndsmobile'- and lay down to sleep until we turned into our road. He immediately jumped up to look out of the window. How he knew he was home I still to this day have no idea!

Once indoors he made himself at home by investigating the garden and leaving his pee-mail to ward off any cats and foxes.

We decided that a name change was definitely needed as he did not look like an Adam, he didn't answer to Adam, and who calls their dog Adam?

Following a family discussion where lots of names were suggested but none approved, discussion on his history with the in-laws resulting in someone saying, 'He's a Taffy then,' as in the nickname for a Welsh person. Up went the ears and he looked over at that person. So, having picked his own name, Taffy he became!

Whilst out at work one day, Taffy managed to reach past the blockade on the kitchen work surface which resulted in him eating a packet of Dentastix, various packets of dog treats, half a loaf of bread, a Tupperware of bird seed, and he also attempted to eat his way through the bag of complete dog food given to us by Battersea. This resulted in a very poorly dog, forty-eight hours of pooping birdseed, and me learning that everything needed to be put out of reach, behind cupboard doors, or way up high where a stool was required to reach.

A Google search for ear tattoos introduced me to the Greyhound Data website where I established that Taffy's racing name was Jazz Night, he was born in the year 2000, had raced thirteen times at Wimbledon and Milton Keynes, and won two races. According to a friend who read the race analysis on his profile, Taffy was disqualified from his last race for fighting!

In the time I had him Taffy didn't show any signs of

aggression, however when he decided to run alongside his Rhodesian ridgeback friend, Hugo, he made some growling sounds, so I think the other dog he supposedly fought with in the race misread the signals.

Taffy was a clever dog; he gave up trying to chase squirrels on-lead as I would dig my heels in and not move until he stopped, which meant I built up enough trust to let him go off-lead. After chasing a squirrel off-lead in the woods one day - where the squirrel doubled back and up a tree - Taffy's front end stopped but the rest of him carried on and he ended up doing a somersault - like something out of a Tom and Jerry cartoon - which resulted in the well known greyhound scream of death, and one dog feeling very sore and sorry for himself.

Taffy was tuned into me, he knew if I was feeling a bit down and would stand in front of me with a gentle nudge and tail wag for me to stroke him. He had his favourite dog walker friends in the park and would always go up and say hello to them.

Taffy loved his share of human food. Fat Friday meant take-away day and kebab meat became known as dog-crack as his eyes looked like they were popping out of his head as he reached out for a share in our meal. If he was lucky, he and William - who joined us about twelve months later - would have a box of donner meat to share - although I did make it last a couple of meals - as a treat. Ice-creams were also a favourite, especially licking the last of a Magnum off the stick. The only problem was that as he'd had twenty teeth removed, the drool ran down my fingers, and once, as I tried to get a better grip, he gave an extra good lick and the stick disappeared in the blink of an eye. Two days later it re-appeared, having passed through his body, and it's now nick-named 'the poo on a stick incident.'

We had a wedding to attend one weekend, which meant Taffy had to go into kennels. Having left him in the capable hands of a greyhound friend, he walked away from me in a sulk, giving me such a look of disgust that I felt guilty leaving him. He didn't eat, and sulked the whole weekend. When I collected him, he stood next to the kennel hand and wouldn't come to me. It was only when I'd pulled up on our drive that he sat up and looked out of the window, and you could see it dawn on him that he had come home. A few weeks later, he was back at the kennels for a week's holiday and this time he came back and nudged/licked my hand through the bars as if to say, 'I'm ok here, and I know you'll be back for me soon.'

Vacuuming the sofas became a competition between me and Taffy. As soon as I started removing the cushions, Taffy would get between me and the sofa and swish his tail gently, waiting for me to take the nozzle out as he wanted to be cleaned too. Having such fine fur, Taffy didn't moult much, but when he did, it would shake off him in clouds. I started vacuuming him when the moulting was really bad - greyhounds don't moult I was told, yeah right! And he loved it so much he would take the opportunity any chance he could get!

In early February 2011, one cold morning, Taffy didn't appear to be himself. A trip to the local vets resulted in emergency surgery to remove an enlarge spleen and his stomach had also torsioned around it. We brought him home that evening with advice that if there were any problems, to take him to the emergency out of hours vets twenty minutes drive away, but there was no way Taffy was going there. He went back to the vets the next morning and walked unaided into the surgery, shocking the vet and her staff who expected him to be carried in. The biopsy results on his spleen came back clear, although the lab asked if the dog was still alive having lost that amount of blood from the enlarged spleen. Whilst recovering, Taffy came to work with me and enjoyed lying on the floor watching colleagues walk past the office. He even decided whilst I was on the phone, to go investigating without me.

Unfortunately Taffy had further complications following this, he constantly needed to go in the garden to toilet, didn't appear to have sensation in his tail, and night after night kept waking me up to go out. After six weeks - with our vet's approval - we decided to take Taffy to the greyhound specialist vets in Edenbridge.

Unfortunately the prognosis wasn't good, and although not obvious from further tests and x-rays, all the symptoms pointed to a tissue tumour, so on 10 March 2011, we made the decision to free Taffy from his pain and let him run free at the Rainbow Bridge.

*

I love the wording from the following saying, and having lost my second greyhound William to cancer – lymphoma - and adopted greyhounds three and four, in time this will be me…

'It came to me that every time I lose a dog; they take a piece of my heart with them. And every new dog that comes into my life gifts me with a piece of their heart. If I live long enough, all the components of my heart will be dog, and I will become as generous and loving as they are.'

Marley's Story – Victoria Hanman

Several times as year, I dog sit a boisterous German shepherd called Max. As much as my greyhound Sylvia rolls her eyes at him and tries to keep him in check, her attitude would change when Max went home and she would become a little subdued for a few days.

Sylvia and I had been with each other for six years when I decided that there was room on the living room floor and in my heart for one more.

However, there were two issues:

1. Sylvia is a total and utter princess who usually has a dislike for other dogs.

2. My partner Tim didn't want another greyhound. Or at least he didn't think he wanted another greyhound!

The first hurdle to was to get round Tim. Sitting together in front of the TV one night, I asked him, just for arguments sake, to put together a 'wish list' for another greyhound, not that I had any intentions of getting another grey -cough cough. His list was -

A boy.

Blue.

Submissive - so Sylvia could boss him around.

Within a twenty mile radius of where we lived.

Cat friendly.

To me this list seemed a difficult one, you don't seem to find many blue greyhounds, and usually they're rehomed quite quickly.

However, Google's a magical tool, and within ten minutes, I'd found a greyhound meeting Tim's requirement down to a T!

I worried how Sylvia would react. She was my baby and she enjoyed having us all to herself. Was I doing the right thing? Would she think that we no longer loved her? Would she feel pushed out?

Marley was a three-year-old retired Irish greyhound. I called the rehoming centre immediately. The following day all three of us set off to meet him. When we arrived at the kennels, there he was. The body of a greyhound but with a broken soul. Marley stayed at the back of the kennel while his boisterous kennel mate took all the lime light.

We took Marley out for a walk with Sylvia - who wasn't overly keen on the idea. Marley had no spirit; he was living, existing but nothing else. He didn't want to be touched, and flinched if he was. He was so nervous and had lost all enthusiasm for the world. Even on a beautiful walk through the countryside, he kept his head down, just trudging along. It was heart breaking.

After the walk, we let Sylvia and Marley off together in the rehoming centre's paddock to see how they got along. Sylvia was playing and jumping around in the long grass, but Marley walked straight back to the gate to go into his kennel.

The rehoming centre staff told us that Marley was originally from Ireland but was found at a greyhound auction in England eighteen months previously. A buyer at the auction had seen Marley in the corner, shaking, cowering and soiling himself. Knowing that the ultimate fate of the dog wouldn't be good, the man had bought Marley for a measly amount and taken him straight to the rehoming centre. This had never been done before.

During the eighteen months in the rehoming centre kennels, the staff had worked with Marley to build his confidence. He'd had Reiki treatments to try and relieve his stress.

I cried when I left him at the kennels that afternoon. That poor broken boy; what had happened to him in his short little life?

On the way home, I told Tim that Marley would be coming home with us one day soon. No ifs, buts or maybes!

I called the centre and arranged a home visit, which we passed with flying colours a few days later.

I arranged to collect Marley the following Thursday. Everything was set to bring my boy home!

The next day the rehoming centre rang me. They'd changed their minds. As far as they were concerned Marley was a special needs dog who would have to stay in the rehoming centre till the end of his days.

As I put the phone down, tears streamed down my face. How could this happen? I hated the thought of Marley being stuck in kennels for one more night, let alone for the rest of his life.

That night I cried and cried, I couldn't understand why this was happening. The following day I called the centre back. I explained that if there was anywhere in the world where Marley would be happiest, it would be in our home. Our home is quite, calm and relaxing, just what a nervous dog like Marley needed.

The man at the rehoming centre again refused to let Marley come home, he instead told me about all the other wonderful greyhounds that needed homes. I told him Marley was the only greyhound for us.

The man finally agreed that Marley could come home with us on Thursday, and again, the night before, they called and cancelled. I sobbed with frustration, the torture was unbearable. Marley was scared and alone in the world and my instincts were to protect him.

The following day I rang the centre again. I was giving up on ever bringing Marley home. I told them that I would do whatever was needed to get him home.

The manager said I would need to visit Marley every day for two weeks to get him used to me. So every day, I travelled the forty mile round trip to see my boy. It was tough and time consuming, and to be honest, I don't think Marley gave two hoots about me. Humans, as far as he was concerned, were definitely not to be trusted.

Finally it was agreed that come hell or high water, that Thursday we would fetch Marley and bring him home forever.

I was so excited, but again, I was nervous that they'd cancel on me again. I wasn't sure if I could take much more.

We travelled to the homing centre and collected Marley. That weekend the centre called to see how Marley was getting on. They asked if on Monday, Marley could be retuned back to them, then we could collect him again the following Thursday to bring him home. I refused point blank and explained how well he was settling in and that sending him back would confuse and upset him. This was his home now. That was the last I ever heard from them.

At home, Marley's fear of humans became much more noticeable. His eyes were like saucers for weeks. He sought sanctuary in the smallest spaces possible. He refused to let us touch him, only maybe if we sat on the floor with our arm stretched at full length.

For eight months, Marley would wake up in the night, screaming, no doubt having nightmares. I would end up on the bedroom floor soothing him back to sleep.

It was apparent that Marley had lived a life full of fear and terror, and from his lumpy bumpy bones - which had possibly been broken and not healed properly - numerous scars and missing ear ends, he'd been badly beaten. As Tim gently stroked Marley all over, tears filled his eyes, how could anyone do this to such a beautiful boy?

His behaviour was destructive; nothing was safe, and we had some really fraught moments. He also didn't grasp the toilet training.

But over time, Marley's eyes began to soften, and his trust in us slowly grew. Every day I would try to desensitise his body to being stroked, to show him that when humans touched him it wasn't a bad thing, and if he wanted, he could enjoy being stroked.

Slowly and gently I'd touch his head and neck, then after a few months his legs and his back, and finally after one long year I could touch him all over without him flinching. He finally let his guard down and started to enjoy being touched.

His behaviour improved too. He stopped destroying everything in his path, apart from the odd pair of shoes or TV remote control.

Marley is now a bonkers little boy. I have never known a dog be so pleased with the simple things in life.

In the mornings, he wakes up from his bed - which is next to my bed on the floor – and he bounces around, his tail going crazy. It's like he's missed me so much and he's just happy to be alive.

He goes crazy when it's his walkies, and does a great Tigger impression when it's dinner time - bouncing up and down on the spot - but he also loves it when it's bedtime and can't get up to bed quick enough. When running around the house like a loon, he's the softest, gentlest soul who just loves cuddles and to be near us, and he's gone from being wary of Tim initially, to being a real daddy's boy.

It's a joy seeing Marley so happy, and what's more surprising, is the love that Sylvia has for him. Sylvia's taken her role as big sister very seriously and keeps an eye on him. The pair seem to have a real connection; when one shakes or stretchers, the other copies. They even lay on their beds the same way!

Recently we discussed if we would take on another special needs case and even though it's been tougher than I ever imagined, and Marley's still making progress, we would do it all over again, just to see those sparkling eyes and wagging tail.

Perry's Story – Joanna Albon

Having wanted a dog for a long time, the opportunity presented itself when I got a job locally, which meant I could come home at lunchtime.

My husband Richard had a colleague who had - amongst her pack of dogs - a greyhound. I'd had many conversations with a customer in Halifax about the whippets she rescued, but the few greyhounds we'd seen always seemed depressed or, if they belonged to one of our neighbours, were trying to kill my dad's dog.

So we decided to take an older dog in case our initial opinion of greyhounds proved correct. How wrong could we be?

We looked on the Greyhound Rescue West of England website and picked out a large fawn and white boy aged ten. Having passed our home check, we went to the wilds of Gloucestershire to collect him.

A tall, self-possessed dog strolled down the path towards us. This was Perry. He acknowledged Richard, but didn't give me a second glance. During the five years he was with us, I was always far less interesting than any male. I quickly learned my place!

Our first walk established that on meeting another dog, he would attack first and ask questions later. He disliked dogs that stared, and hated Old English Sheepdogs with a passion. He even attacked a three-month-old collie puppy once.

We never did resolve his fear aggression issues, though he was fine with visiting dogs; he just pretended they weren't there.

I took him clicker training. Unfortunately he couldn't handle the hall floor very well but we did enough to get started. I would do some training with him on every walk. In fact, if he thought we'd gone more than half way without some treats on offer, he would nudge me. If he could have coughed, he would.

During a thunderstorm, Perry discovered the upstairs, a refuge under the stairs to the attic, and our bed. Lucky it was king-size, just enough room for Richard, Perry and me on the very edge. Well, greyhounds do like to stretch out!

More than once, having got up in the night, I ended up sleeping across the bottom of the bed.

Then I got tougher. On holiday in Scotland, I went up the first night to find Richard and Perry both fast asleep, Perry in my place. He would not wake up, so I gently rotated him and tipped him off the edge of the bed. He never refused to move again.

Unfortunately we couldn't let Perry off lead in places we didn't know as he had a tendency to follow his own route, no matter how many treats were on offer. But as he got older we could let him off more, because we could run faster than he would trot.

For a large, ungainly, old dog he could be surprisingly agile and strong. He was a bin raider extraordinaire. One evening we came in to discover he had eaten six eggs and half a pound of clotted cream. He had a cast iron stomach. Another time he managed to open a sealed tin of chocolates, which he kindly shared with Lizzy - we had three greyhounds by this time; one is never enough.

For a couple of days afterwards, they excreted chocolate scented poo. Lizzy squeaked each time as she passed the wrappers, but Perry was made of sterner stuff.

Numerous jackets were pulled off the coat hooks if ripping the pockets out didn't reveal unused treats. Perry even broke a couple of the hooks. Of course, once I'd made the mistake of leaving treats in a pocket, dog logic stated that every coat must contain treats!

Perry never lost his fear of loud noises, but arnica would send him to sleep and he would stay hidden until the danger had passed. We discovered skullcap and valerian for bonfire night, which he sailed through as a result. The effect even lasted to the New Year fireworks. Gun firing on the moor, or even someone using a hammer, would result in him refusing to leave the house or legging it back home.

Heavy rain predicted thunderstorms and, since we have quite a lot of precipitation on Dartmoor that caused some problems.

He didn't like the dark either, and would spend his time like Walker in Dad's Army, staring suspiciously at bushes, trees and behind him.

As he grew older, Perry slept a lot more. He still loved his walks and sometimes he would want to walk a lot further than me. He would quite often get up to greet Richard, but I just got a head lift - sometimes not even that - and a slight movement of the ears and eyes to indicate he was pleased to see me. Rather like our current twosome, Pluto and Misty, in fact.

Any rabbit careless enough to disregard him regretted it, and he found hens fascinating. A movement in the distance required investigation, particularly if it was canine. He also had a good nose and would drag Richard through the woods on the track of deer.

I have abiding memories of people smiling when they saw him, Perry not believing his luck at seeing rabbits at motorway services, and laughing as he dragged Richard down sand dunes.

Perry was our first greyhound; we are now on numbers six and seven.

He started our love affair with the breed and taught us how graciously greyhounds accept cuddles, that beds are for them, how gentle, easy going and adaptable they are, how it is worth the wait for their personalities to show, and why would anyone ever want any other dog? Lurchers and other sighthounds are good too as they have similar personalities.

George's Story – Ann Waghorn

We adopted our first greyhound in 2007. We already had a Labrador, ten-year-old Kizzy, and wanted another dog as a companion for her. We chose a greyhound as we felt that their laid back temperament would suit that of an equally laid back Labrador.

My husband had grown up with greyhounds because his father owned and trained them. Some of the dogs were kept at home - more like family pets than racing dogs - and he's always loved these goofy gentle giants.

Following discussions with our local Retired Greyhound Trust re-homing kennels, we went along to meet the dogs with Kizzy in tow. It was essential that she and whichever hound we rehomed got on with each other and it took several weeks before we decided that George was the right dog for us.

When we first met George, he was very thin and his coat was in poor condition. The kennels told us that he'd been homed for two years when he finished racing, but that he'd then been found roaming the streets, was picked up by the local warden and taken to the pound, where they wait seven days for someone to claim them.

George - who was only six and a half - was just one day away from being put to sleep when a lady at the pound rang the kennels to enquire if they could take him. Luckily they had room.

George settled in very well with us and he got on extremely well with Kizzy. She was a very maternal dog and taught him a lot of things, such as how to play with toys. He had no idea what toys were, or what a dog chew was. He would stare disdainfully at it, wondering what to do.

Most greyhounds are afraid of thunderstorms and George was no exception to this. Kizzy sat with him comforting him during a storm, and it was lovely to see them together. In return he protected her on walks, and when she went blind, he became her eyes. He would walk very slowly by her side and wait patiently for her to catch up.

Although he settled in well, it took a year before he came up to us for a cuddle; he seemed to keep his distance at first, as though he was afraid to love us in case he got hurt again.

We had some wonderful years with the two dogs; we took them on holiday on our boat, and camping. If they couldn't go, we wouldn't go.

George loved it all, but he would get a bit nervous when we were packing to go home, it was as if he was wondering if we were going to abandon him.

Kizzy went to the Rainbow Bridge at the age of fifteen. She suffered a stroke and George was by her side, comforting her, while we sought help. We worried that he was going to pine for her, but he seemed to cope without her.

Eighteen months later, he became unwell. His illness coincided with Bonfire Night and we thought it was the fireworks that were upsetting him as he was terrified of them. The vet gave him some tablets to calm him, but they had no effect. He didn't get better whatever we did and we tried everything we could with the vet's help, but he went downhill fast.

A few days before he crossed to the Rainbow Bridge, I was cuddling him and he chattered his teeth at me. He'd never done that before. I didn't know what it meant at the time and just thought he was cold. I now know that it's a greyhound's way of saying, 'I love you.'

We were heartbroken to lose two beautiful dogs within a short space of time, so we decided that we couldn't go through the heartache again, and wouldn't have another dog.

However, fate took matters into its own hands.

We went to the kennels to donate some things and the kennel manager said, 'I've got just the dog for you.'

With that, Paddy came to the door to say hello. The manager got him out and we were smitten! We went back the next week to take him out for a walk and that was it, we adopted him there and then.

I'm so glad that we went to the kennels that day, as we now have another goofy gentle giant, who loves everyone and everything.

He is so different to George - not afraid of thunderstorms or fireworks. He loves it when the children next door are in the garden as he likes to run up and down the lawn when he sees them through the fence, and then he'll run indoors as if they are chasing him!

He likes to pinch things as well, and you'll often find items that he's taken, on his bed.

I don't think now that we could ever not have a dog, and I'd love to have a greyhound and a Labrador together again as they complement each other so well.

Sulley's Story – Michelle White

I'd never seen a greyhound before, until I met the lovely lady who is now my mother-in-law, Pauline. She was the owner of two beautiful brindle ex-racing greyhounds, Halva (HELUA) and Boris. I was a dog walker at the time, and I spotted these two skinny, but quite elegant looking dogs walking down my road, so I ran up to the lady and got chatting to her about them.

A month later we'd become good friends and as time went by I fell in love with her dogs, and eventually her son, Andy, who is now my husband.

I moved in with them and decided to get us a dog. By this time, I was working locally as a veterinary nurse, and we used to work with the greyhound training kennels at Biggin Hill in Kent once a week.

One day I was asked to go with the vet to the kennels to do our weekly checkups on the dogs, and they looked so adorable I just fell in love with them all. I asked the trainer if there were any white dogs needing a home. He said he had one, a two and a half-year-old boy, who was very cute, but he wasn't a great racer so he'd been retired. I asked the trainer to put him on reserve, as he now had a home with us.

Sulley - as he was called - was due to race that weekend, but I said, 'NO WAY! He doesn't need to run any more for his life; he now has a loving family, a forever sofa, and a lovely greyhound, Auntie Halva, waiting for him.' Halva came from the same kennels, as did Boris, but he'd sadly died by then, due to spinal cancer. A couple of years after Boris went to the bridge, we lost Halva, to cancer of the shoulder.

We ended up bringing Sulley home on the 6 October 2002, a few days after I'd found out sadly that I'd lost a baby. I didn't even know that I was eight weeks pregnant until it was too late. So in a way, Sulley became that baby to me. If we hadn't brought Sulley home with us, I can honestly say that I wouldn't be here now.

I still remember when we went to get Sulley from the kennels. I remember seeing this white and fawn teenage hooligan with a wonky ear and a chunk of his tongue missing, he was all muscle then, and very bouncy. He reminded me of tiger from Winnie the Pooh, lol!

He came home with us, and at first I admit he was hard work, but we took it all in our stride and coped well. It took us six years to calm him down and desensitize him from what he'd learned at the training kennels. As I used to work at the vets, in a way he became my patient. I helped with his castration - under supervision - brought him back home to recover and everything went ok.

A couple of years after Sulley lived with us, he decided to poison himself. We had rats in the garden because the neighbours used to feed the birds, so we put rat poison underneath our summer house, making sure everything was out of Sulley's reach, but we didn't think he'd get hold of the poisoned rat. My mother-in-law found him playing with what she thought was his toy, but when the rat squealed she realised something was wrong.

She called me, and I rushed down the stairs as fast as I could, grabbed the baby wipes, and cleaned Sulley's mouth to make sure he wasn't bleeding. Thank goodness the blood wasn't his, it was the rat's! I put the rat in a bag - by this stage it was dead -and drove straight to my vet.

If we'd left it a bit longer, he'd most definitely have died of rat poisoning. I'm so glad my veterinary nursing background kicked into action that day! My boss told me that if I'd waited five more minutes we'd have lost him. Thank goodness he was insured as the bill was over £2k!

At the age of six, he was diagnosed with a grade three heart murmur, and at aged twelve he got gastroenteritis and colitis, and we nearly lost him twice, but the vet saved him. He was very accident prone, but we still loved him.

Sulley wasn't just a dog to me, the way I see it, we rescued each other! I rescued him from the horrible training kennels, and he rescued me from having lost my baby. I guess all the love and maternal feelings that I had for the baby were passed down to Sulley. I could never thank him enough for helping me get over the loss. To me he was a great support, he was my rock, we helped each other, and we were there for each other in the good and bad times and up to his last breath.

We used to take him everywhere we went; he was my little furry shadow. If there was a place where Sulley wouldn't be allowed, I wouldn't go in. I'm so glad we managed to take him to the seaside for his ninth birthday. We always used to celebrate his birthday with a big party and lots of treats - doggie cakes etc. My friends used to bring him pressies too, and a few doggie friends for Sulley - after all it was his birthday!

He lived with us in our flat after we moved out of my in-laws house, then Andy proposed and we got married in June 2008. Sulley couldn't come to the actual service, but he joined us at the reception. We decided to have it at home, so he could be part of our special day, and celebrate it with us.

He was always so gentle, trusting, loyal, very loving and liked to play hide and seek. He would adapt to any situation immediately, I couldn't fault him, he was a very special boy. We used to go on big walks, sometimes just walking for miles. He loved walking and doing his zoomies round the park. We took him to a lot of places.

He was a very well behaved boy, even though he wasn't properly socialized. I was intrigued by what was going on in his mind, and he gave me the push I needed to study dog psychology, just so I could understand him better. He was the one that made Paw Buddys – our pet sitting service – happen.

We are so immensely grateful and lucky to have had Sulley in our lives for thirteen awesome years. Unfortunately due to his osteoarthritis, he started to go downhill very quickly. He wasn't able to stand for long periods of time, he wasn't enjoying his walks; he was losing weight very quickly and also losing his balance, so we had to make the awful but kind decision of letting him go.

We decided to take him back home to my in-laws - getting in the car to make our way to my in-laws took forever – he'd lived there with us for over eight years, it was also a place he knew as home. He had an amazing fifteenth birthday weekend/ send off party. He spent the day in the garden with most of the people that mattered to him. His daddy Andy, his paternal grandma, Pauline, his little sister Lilly – a lurcher - and my sister-in-law Leila, a spaniel - my in-laws' dog - Uncle Steve and Aunty Torie, my best friend and his girlfriend, and uncle Martin my husband's best mate. On the Saturday we had a professional family photo shoot done.

We said goodbye to our sweet granddad on Friday 13 April 2015 at 3.30 pm. I used to think Friday 13ths were lucky for me until then. We'd celebrated Lilly's birthday the day before too. Rikus, our vet, came to the house - we were having cuddles and saying our goodbyes as Rikus arrived. Sulley had spent the day on his bed in the garden having a nice sun bath. We gave him a massive treat of all the things he wasn't allowed to eat.

Rikus and the vet nurse joined us in the garden, and everyone else went into the house as they'd already said goodbye to Sulley. While the vet was getting ready to put Sulley to sleep, I put my forehead on his, held his head between my hands and talked to him. I thanked him for saving me, and for everything he'd done for us in the time he'd spent with us. I couldn't thank him enough. I gave him lots of kisses and cuddles, trying to hold my tears back, and by the time I lifted my head from his, I knew he was gone. It was very peaceful for him.

I don't know how I managed to keep it together though. I guess I didn't want him to know that I was upset; I didn't want him to die knowing that we were heartbroken about having to let him go. I used my dog psychology skills on him, and me, that day.

I asked Rikus if he'd definitely gone, he said yes, and then I just lost it. I'd managed to hold it together for Sulley's sake. I thought that I would be worse than I was. I guess it was shock.

We wrapped him up in his blanket, I carried him to the vet's car, said my final goodbye and off he went. He was cremated and came back home to us two weeks later in his little casket. He now has his own shrine in our front room and we light a candle for him every night. It still isn't easy to do, and as I feel he left a big hole our family.

However, that hole is slowly being filled by Lilly. She joined us on the 1 June 2013 aged fourteen months. We got her from Celia Cross Greyhound Trust, a rescue close to my heart as I first heard of them when I worked at the vets.

Angel - as Lilly was named in the kennels - was the youngest of a litter of six gorgeous pups - two boys and four girls. Their mother was due to give birth when she was taken into the rescue kennels, and I followed every Facebook post regarding her and the pups.

When the pups were just ten-days old we went to meet them, but obviously they were too young to be handled, so I had to wait till they were a bit older.

Lilly was adopted when she was ten-weeks old, but due to a change in circumstances from her previous owner, she was returned to the kennels. I was told she'd been returned and immediately phoned to ask if she could be reserved as we'd definitely be interested in giving her a forever sofa.

After a month of contact, the day finally came for us to collect her, and she's been with us ever since. The previous adopters had called her Yuki, but we changed her name to Lilly. Having her around has really helped us deal with Sulley's departure. I'd love to one day have a bond with her in the same way I had with Sulley and we are getting there, slowly. I believe she was sent our way for a reason...to be our little angel, to help us cope with Sulley's loss.

We still miss him terribly; words cannot express how much we love him. Sulley, you were my saviour and I will ALWAYS love you and be grateful for that. You were one in a million.
RIP SWEET BOY, HOPE TO SEE YOU AGAIN ONE DAY.
LOVE YOU BABY. SULLEY WHITE 08.03.2000 – 13.04.2015

Remember Me – Tina K Burton.

Remember me when the sun shines; remember me in the rain,
Remember all our happy times, when I was free from pain.
Remember when you took me home, that very special day?
You said it was forever, you promised I could stay.
We had so much fun together, long walks, and cuddles too,
I never needed very much, as long as I had you.
Remember all those moments, the memories we made,
They'll help to keep you smiling, and my face will never fade.
I'll be with you forever; we'll never be apart,
Although you cannot see me now, I'm right there, in your heart.